FISHER AND CUNNINGHAM

By the same author

The Escape of Charles II
Man of War: Sir Robert Holmes and the Restoration Navy
Pepys: a Biography
This War without an Enemy: a History of the English Civil Wars
The Image of the King: Charles I and Charles II
An English Education: a Perspective of Eton
Clarendon and his Friends

FISHER
&
CUNNINGHAM

A Study in the Personalities
of the Churchill Era

Richard Ollard

CONSTABLE · LONDON

First published in Great Britain 1991
by Constable and Company Limited
3 The Lanchesters, 162 Fulham Palace Road
London W6 9ER
Copyright © 1991 by Richard Ollard
The right of Richard Ollard to be
identified as the author of this Work
has been asserted by him in accordance
with the Copyright, Designs and Patents Act 1988
ISBN 0 09 470490 2
Set in Monophoto Sabon 11pt by
Servis Filmsetting Limited, Manchester
Printed in Great Britain by
St Edmundsbury Press Limited
Bury St Edmunds, Suffolk

A CIP catalogue record for this book
is available from the British Library

Contents

Acknowledgements

My greatest debt, apart from that acknowledged in the dedication, is to Sir Michael Culme-Seymour who urged me to write about A. B. Cunningham while men who had known him in his hour could still recall him. To him and to Admiral Royer Dick, two survivors from the imperishable days in the Mediterranean, I am principally obliged for whatever sense of a living personality I have managed to convey. Others on whose recollections I have drawn are acknowledged in the text.

My thanks are due to the Trustees of the British Library and to the Master, Fellows and Scholars of Churchill College in the University of Cambridge for permission to quote from manuscripts in their possession and to Random Century Ltd for permission to quote from Lord Cunningham's memoirs, *A Sailor's Odyssey*.

Sources

Much of the original material for the study of Fisher is in print. I have therefore, in writing about him, cited references. With Cunningham the opposite is true. The main documentary source is his papers in the British Library. There is also much of value in the collections of the Archive Centre at Churchill College, Cambridge. Quotation, when it is not from his autobiography, *A Sailor's Odyssey*, or otherwise attributed, is from one of these two sources and I do not think a reader who wishes to examine its context will find any difficulty in tracing the original. The Navy Records Society hopes shortly to publish an edition of his papers. As will also be clear, I have drawn freely on personal information supplied by those who served on his staff or, more remotely, under his command.

I am aware that this procedure lacks consistency, but am comforted by the reflection that both Admirals, widely as they differed, were at one in not setting much value on this quality.

Introduction

Since Trafalgar every naval career of distinction has been lived *sub specie Nelsonitatis*. Nelson not only provides a pattern of achievement unrivalled in any profession for its dramatic appositeness and effect. He personifies an attitude, a spirit, that has the supreme advantage of being at once easy to identify and impossible to define. Above all he is intensely human, exemplifying virtues that are never remote and weaknesses that are all too sympathetic. His power of attraction, overwhelming in his lifetime, still shines steadily through a hundred biographies.

That light is reflected, that fame echoed, in the biographies and epitaphs of the naval commanders of our own century. When Admiral Sir Bernard Rawlings, a fighting leader with a record of high distinction, chose the inscription for his own tombstone it was, simply, 'One of Cunningham's Captains'. The reference to the Nelsonic 'Band of Brothers' is unmistakable. Stephen Roskill, whose history *The War at Sea 1939–1945* still bestrides the field, wrote after Cunningham's death that 'He was without superior as a sea commander in World War II and with his gaiety, indomitability and aggressive spirit was in the Nelson tradition.'

In the case of Jacky Fisher the Nelsonic invocation was almost inevitable. He was certainly the first naval officer since Nelson to make anything approaching a comparable impact on the national consciousness. In spite of his provocative and well-publicized contempt for tradition and continuity – 'History is the record of exploded ideas' – he took good care to establish his own Nelsonic provenance. He was fond of characterizing his schemes of reform as possessing the four Nelsonic attributes: 'the habits of mind required for fighting people, self-reliance, fertility of resource, fearlessness of responsibility and the power of initiative'. He lost no opportunity of pointing out that he had been nominated to a cadetship in 1854 by Admiral Sir William Parker, the last surviving officer on the Navy List to have served under Nelson, and that the first ship on whose books he had been entered was the *Victory* herself. He habitually, though inaccurately, claimed to have taken office as First Sea Lord on Trafalgar Day, 21 October.

Cunningham's professional achievement bears at first sight more points of resemblance to Nelson's. His great victories shone the brighter for being won in a war that on land had grown darker and darker. As Commander-in-Chief in the Mediterranean he found his mind retracing Nelson's steps: 'Waking or sleeping, Malta is always in my thoughts.'* Most obviously he shared with Nelson the opportunities and responsibilities, denied to Fisher, of command-ing a fleet in a great war.

Both men shaped their concepts, formed their standards, measured their aspirations, even to a degree modelled their conduct on their understanding of Nelson. Their admirers have naturally accepted these values. Indeed it would be perverse not to do so since the Royal Navy, however different it may have been in the periods during which the two served, was unquestionably inspired by the image of Nelson and kept, as it still keeps, Trafalgar Day as the greatest feast in the naval calendar. Yet the two were, at even the most superficial glance, very, very different men. How far both or either in their essential nature resembled their hero is another question still. Manifestly, all three were outstanding masters of the naval profession. Manifestly, all three had powers of attraction, of inspiration, of leadership that were unforgettable. Mercifully, all

* Perhaps a loose recollection of Nelson's letter to Sir James Erskine, 26 October 1799: 'I am in desperation about Malta – we shall lose it, I am afraid, past redemption.'

three were highly articulate. One can always see at once what they were saying – and what they were saying was always interesting and often challenging. Indeed in Fisher's case it was always pungent and often witty. None of them came from rich or aristocratic families. All had a strong sense of religion and an even stronger sense of dedication to the navy.

The differences between them, their individuality considered in relation to each other, will form the subject of this book. Its impulse is that of the biographer or perhaps more strictly the portraitist. What Dr Johnson called the 'anfractuosities of the human mind' are its concern rather than the trajectories of shells, the performance of the Mark IV Argo clock or the myriad technicalities of naval warfare that made the world of Fisher and Cunningham so much more uncertain a place than Nelson's. Clearly the impact of these developments on the two men, more especially their reaction to them, will assert itself. Fisher was an enthusiast for gadgetry, Cunningham dourly resistant to it. Yet both men were at one in their emphatic and often-repeated view that the human element was all, beside which the mechanical and scientific assistance at their disposal was to be counted, in Cromwell's phrase, 'but dung and dross'. An author may thus plausibly pre-empt their approval of a study of their own personalities that sails under its own colours. Too much pains have been spent on taking people out of history: it is time that they were put back in.

The two men are unequally represented on the library shelves, except in the purely arithmetical sense that each wrote a volume of memoirs and both have been the subject of more than one biography. Cunningham's autobiography though long is only fitfully informative. The two biographies of him by Oliver Warner (1967) and S. W. C. Pack (1974) though sound and useful do not quite rise to the level of their subject. The volumes of Stephen Roskill's official history *The War at Sea* (1954–1961) give by far the best account of the battles he fought and the services he rendered in the highest commands from 1939 to 1945.

With Fisher the case is quite the opposite. His own notably brief

Memories (1919) and *Records* (1919) convey in every line the strong flavour of their writer's personality. The modern biography by Ruddock Mackay (1973) is penetrating, balanced and scholarly. But it is the *oeuvre* of a remarkable American historian, Professor Arthur Marder, that has raised Fisher to an eminence comparable to that of Pepys or Anson and has brought his mind and his mischief into the common currency of reference and allusion. His impishness and originality have communicated themselves, thanks largely to Marder, to a public who are generally ignorant of their naval inheritance and of the exhilaration and vigour of its personalities. The great series *From the Dreadnought to Scapa Flow* tells the history of the Royal Navy in the early twentieth century with a verve and an authority that Fisher himself, the hero of the story, could not have surpassed. The three volumes of his correspondence *Fear God and Dread Nought*, superbly edited, bring him before the reader larger, if possible, than life.

It is no detraction from Professor Marder's achievement to say that his task was made easier by the fact that Fisher was a natural, a compulsive, communicator. He was never happier, never more himself, than when expounding his flow of ideas in speech or on paper. He loved publicity. He cultivated the leading journalists of his time with the ardour of a lover. To Cunningham on the other hand any such thing was anathema. He hated the press. He disdained even favourable publicity. His cult of the Silent Service verged on the Trappist. Small wonder then that three or four people seem to have some idea of Fisher for every one from whom the name of Cunningham elicits a sign of recognition. Yet it is Cunningham's bust, not Fisher's, that shares the watch with Nelson in Trafalgar Square.

The continuity of great institutions deceives the historical eye at the same time as it adds a dimension to historical understanding. The naval officers in *Persuasion* will seem familiar to any reader of wide naval acquaintance. Nelson's navy with its wooden ships and towering spread of canvas seems, on the material plane, worlds away. Yet, as has been pointed out, Fisher, the champion of the dreadnought and the battle-cruiser, prized his direct personal connection with it. The link with Cunningham is obviously closer. Fisher, as Second Sea Lord, signed Cunningham's commission in 1903. The navy that he was transforming was the navy in which the great admiral of the second war held his first commands.

Chronology is a map of history that is not drawn to scale. Cunningham, in many ways, perhaps stood closer to Nelson than Fisher did. Certainly he entered the navy at a time when its supremacy in the world and its place in the British scheme of things was an article of national faith. To attempt to put a value on it, to examine, to criticize, to question what it was and what it could or should do, was widely felt to be subversive, if not blasphemous. The navy as it actually existed embodied the idea of seapower as the guarantee of our freedom, our wealth, our civilization. After 1914–1918 this was no longer true. 'The question was, could the army win the war before the navy lost it?' True or false, fair or unfair, this judgement, unthinkable before 1914, was not only thinkable but widely canvassed. The navy that fought the war of 1939–1945 had lost the privileges, almost the immunities, that call to mind those of the European nobility under the *ancien régime*. Cunningham, who had been formed in the earlier mould, won his victories under a different dispensation. Fisher, who had presided over the navy from which such great things had been expected, had himself entered a service in very low water. He, more than any man, had restored it to the well-found, thoroughly professional condition it had been in when Nelson joined. And yet, and yet . . . he was so utterly unlike a naval officer. Cunningham, on the other hand, could never have been mistaken for anything else.

Of course judgements of this kind reflect the period in which they are made. The historian stands inside history, although by efforts of imagination and the labour of scholarship he can sometimes transcend his condition. The naval officers under whom Fisher served when he was young would have seemed as strange to Nelson as they do to us. Captain Shadwell, a Fellow of the Royal Society no less, urging his men on to a desperate attack on the Peiho forts, armed with an umbrella and wearing a tall hat; Captain Oliver Jones who kept a French chef and a Churchillian supply of champagne to fête his young officers before sending them up to the foretop in full mess dress on some tipsy pretext. If Fisher seems to us a bird of exotic plumage the service in which he grew up might not have thought him so. Let us try to set him in his context.

FISHER

A number of admirals in our history have possessed the gift of expressing themselves in striking and memorable language. Drake's famous letter to Queen Elizabeth and Nelson's prayer written on the night before Trafalgar are almost as well-known as the great sea-fights that occasioned them. Both Nelson himself and his successor and companion-in-arms, Collingwood, wrote letters that expressed their very different minds and personalities with a freshness and a vigour that will always excite the admiration of those who care for good writing.

In this quality no admiral of the past two centuries has surpassed Jacky Fisher. The speed, the punch, the wit of his correspondence delighted its recipients from kings and cabinet ministers to journalists and private friends, and has continued to delight all who study the history of the navy in the enormous period that stretches from the Indian Mutiny to the end of the First World War. When he died in July 1920, full of years and honour as Admiral of the Fleet Lord Fisher of Kilverstone GCB, OM, the Board of Admiralty wrote in their official letter of condolence to his son:

There is no part in the multitudinous activities of modern naval service in which his influence has not been felt. The nation has been fortunate in having at its disposal, during the greatest period of naval development the world has seen, Lord Fisher's unrivalled qualities of untiring zeal, brilliant genius, and whole-

hearted devotion. His remarkable abilities were displayed alike
in the technical development of the fleet and in its appurtenances,
in the training and education of the personnel of the Royal Navy,
and in the strategical disposition of the Sea Forces of the country,
both in preparation for and in actual operations of war, and three
successive Sovereigns and their Ministers have enjoyed the
benefit of his counsels during one of the most critical and eventful
periods of the history of this realm.[1]

Fisher himself would have put it more pungently and more
sardonically but he would not have dissented from the gist. That he
was a genius can hardly be doubted. Quite apart from the testimony
of the Lords Commissioners of the Admiralty, each and all of whom
had, till within a few weeks of his death, smarted under the rope's
end of his criticism – derisive, devastating and delivered with the
gusto of the born controversialist – there is abundant evidence that
some of the best judges outside naval circles thought him so. King
Edward VII, as shrewd in discerning the quality of men as any
public figure of his time, especially valued and supported him. J. L.
Garvin, the greatest political journalist of his contemporaries,
recognized the divine fire that burned in him. Lord Esher, the
eminence grise of the late nineteenth and early twentieth century,
told Fisher early in their acquaintance that there were less than a
dozen people in the country who really counted and that he was
certainly one of them. The leading politicians of his time, Asquith,
Balfour, Lloyd George and Winston Churchill, might doubt his
steadiness of judgement, fear his intemperance of language or
reckon up the cost of co-operating with so tigerish a figure. But they
had no doubt as to his extraordinary powers of mind. In his
combination of the intellectual energy that enabled him to master
complex and technical subjects and the brilliant gifts of exposition
that enabled him to state his conclusions in pithy, forceful and
memorable language he resembled Churchill and F. E. Smith. Like
Churchill he possessed not only a formidable intelligence but a rare
power of imagination. Like Churchill he distrusted compromise

and despised the ordinary, the obvious and the everyday. And like Churchill, for all his gifts of mind, he was first, last and all the time, a man of passion, glorying in the warmth and impulsiveness of his temperament and disparaging the cold flatness of rational analysis. As he wrote in January 1910 to the close woman-friend whom he thought of as his possible biographer:

> Impulse is all with me and I answer on the moment! (Out of the abundance of the heart the mouth speaketh!) Myself I hate a calculated letter or a prepared speech. You can go round the corner and get Buggins or Stiggins to do either for you . . . Whatever success I have had is more attributable to the action of imagination than to the dictates of cold reason. Ruskin was great there and encouraged the building of castles in the air and then the rearing up of the earthly foundations to meet them in the skies.[2]

The literary echoes of this eloquent passage disclose the deepest sources of the Admiral's spirit. He was a fervent, if idiosyncratic, Christian, a churchgoer of devoted assiduity, a passionate lover of the Bible, particularly in the early translations on which the Authorised Version is based, and an admirer of the hymns of John and Charles Wesley.

Fisher's strong religious conviction was the only dominant element in his nature that found no counterpart in Churchill. In every other respect their exceptional qualities matched to a degree and to an extent themselves remarkable. No wonder the two men took to each other with a strength of mutual attraction most uncommon in the relations between a politician and a Service Chief. Fisher in his own words 'fell desperately in love with Winston Churchill. I think he's quite the nicest fellow I ever met and such a quick brain that it's a delight to talk to him.'[3] Churchill, he reported, 'said his penchant for me was that I painted with a big brush! and was violent! I reminded him that even "The Kingdom of Heaven suffereth violence, and the violent take it by force."'[4] It was a marriage of true minds. Nothing else can explain the tenderness and generosity that each showed for the other after each had, in the other's opinion, done all he could to ruin the other's career and to frustrate what each saw as the salvation of their country in her days of danger and disaster.

Both men were alike in one important respect, namely that the training and equipment of their own immensely powerful minds had been left largely to their own efforts. Churchill had, it is true, been a boy at Harrow but by his own account it was in the long solitary hours as a subaltern in India that he formed and furnished his mind. Fisher had not even that slender academic advantage. He went to sea in 1854 at the age of thirteen, nominated, as he loved to remember, to a naval cadetship by the last of Nelson's captains, still on the active list as Commander-in-Chief at Plymouth. His first ship was the *Victory*, still venerably if somewhat shakily in commission. In the following year on his promotion to midshipman he was appointed to the corvette *Highflyer*, then bound for the China station. Four years later he was in the bloody and ineffective action against the forts at the mouth of the Peiho river with which the Second Opium War opened its inglorious annals.

The letters in which he describes these battles are almost the earliest still extant from his pen. They show the same qualities as his mature correspondence. There is no attempt to disguise or underplay the horrors of war or the agonies of the wounded. On the contrary they are depicted in strong colours, indeed with a kind of zest that might be mistaken for heartlessness were it not also plain that the writer really pitied what he saw. But he is too intensely alive not to find such scenes, shocking and revolting as they were, undeniably exciting; and too candid to wish to conceal the fact. These first impressions of war remained present to his consciousness throughout his long life. He never allowed anyone to romanticize the facts of war and went out of his way to emphasize that humanity in war is a contradiction in terms. Violence and terror are of its essence. To play down this primary condition seemed to him either hypocritical and therefore dishonest or else stupid and muddled. The bellicose maxims that he repeated with such evident relish: 'Ruthless, Remorseless and Relentless', 'Moderation in War is Imbecility' and suchlike exemplify this attitude.

That he did not at all regret the loss of what the public schools and universities of his time had to offer is abundantly plain. 'Of all the systems of education ever devised by the wit of man,' he wrote in February 1904 when he was on the eve of his great remodelling of the naval profession, 'nothing approaches or ever can approach the education of the sea in giving self-reliance, fertility of resource, fearlessness of responsibility, and the power of initiative. These four great qualities are the habits of mind required for fighting people, for, as has been truly said, they are the four great Nelsonic attributes, and gales of wind, fog, the imminence of great danger, and the uncertainty of life from hour to hour, all of them conduce unconsciously to train the tender lad to become a brave and resourceful man.'[5] Again and again he reverts to the value of his early training. Nearing the end of the six years as First Sea Lord during which he had transformed the navy both as regards ships and weapons as well as in the career structure of officers and men he wrote '. . . the strange thing is that by far the best part of my life in works and results was as a Midshipman and a Lieutenant. I commanded a ship at 19 [he was in temporary command of the brig *Coromandel*], the day I was 19, and sent on a fighting expedition by myself, and calculated eclipses at 16, and wrote a paper on the dip of the magnetic needle, but everyone in the world believes I was only born on 21 October 1904, when I became First Sea Lord.'*[6]

From such a passage the unwary might infer that Fisher was a die-hard defender of the old ways in the navy, urging the retention of sail for its character-building qualities, maintaining the disciplinary virtues of flogging (as a midshipman he had enthusiastically obtained 36 lashes for a member of his boat's crew who had absented himself while on duty), opposing the introduction of sanitation and the comforts of life as leading to effeminacy and

---

* He had, in fact, become First Sea Lord on 20 October, but the magnetic attraction of Trafalgar Day was too strong.

softness and all the rest of it. Nothing could be further from the truth. Fisher was an out-and-out radical (it was not chance that he got on so famously with Garibaldi while showing him over HMS *Warrior*, the first ironclad, at Portland in 1864). History, he proclaimed, was the record of exploded ideas. To get rid of out-of-date ships, and even more those senior officers who were content with the ideas instilled into them in youth – 'naval fossils' – became his prime objectives. Every new development, the armoured vessel, the all-big-gun ship, the torpedo, the mine, the submarine, the aircraft that he correctly foresaw would transform the nature of sea-fighting, was either pioneered or championed by this extraordinarily versatile and receptive sea officer, who, paradoxically, never ceased to idolize Nelson and to glory in the apprenticeship, hardly changed since Nelson's day, that he had served to his profession. It is the antitheses of Fisher's mentality and of his span of personal experience that make him so conspicuous a figure not only in the history of the Royal Navy in the twentieth century but in the development of modern navies generally. He bridges a gulf, connects the new with the old as no one else quite does. As he wrote of himself when reflecting in old age on his time as Gunnery Lieutenant in the *Warrior*:

It is seldom appreciated – it certainly was not then appreciated on board the 'Warrior' when I was her gunnery Lieutenant – that this, our first armour-clad ship-of-war, the 'Warrior' would cause a fundamental change in what had been in vogue for something like a thousand years! For the Navy that had been founded by Alfred the Great had lasted till then without any fundamental change till came this first Ironclad Battleship. There is absolutely nothing in common between the fleets of Nelson and the Jutland Battle! Sails have given way to steam. Oak to steel. Lofty, four-decked ships with 144 guns like the 'Santissima Trinidad' to low-lying hulls like that of the first 'Dreadnought'. Guns of one hundred tons instead of one ton! And Torpedoes, Mines, Submarines, Aircraft. And then even coal being obsolete!

And, unlike Nelson's day, no human valour can now compensate for mechanical inferiority.[7]

For all the eagerness with which Fisher seized on technical innovations, for all the irreverent glee with which he ridiculed opposition to the mechanization of warfare, he never for a moment made the mistake of thinking that this process diminished the importance of the fighting man or of the qualities required in his officers. Very much the reverse. All his life Fisher did what he could to improve the conditions of service for what he picturesquely called the 'bluejackets'. While he was First Sea Lord this was a very great deal. Terms of service, pay, messing, liability to punishment had already undergone considerable reform since his days as a midshipman but he improved them further. But his main achievement was to increase the opportunities of promotion from the lower deck. The navy of the nineteenth century, like many other British and Continental institutions, took it for granted that advantages of birth were all but prerequisite for positions of command. Fisher's radicalism as well as his professionalism made such assumptions impossible to him. Napoleon and Cromwell were, after Nelson, his great heroes. The Napoleonic concept of '*La carrière ouverte aux talents*' was Fisher's avowed aim. He had seen enough good men shouldered aside by those who had nothing but family connection to recommend them. He had made his own way in the service, often against bitter hostility and personal jealousy, solely by his own talents and industry. He was without the private means that most professional officers either in the army or the navy found necessary to their position. 'I entered the navy penniless, friendless, forlorn' was one of his favourite and most often reiterated descriptions of his early career. The 'fossils' of whom in his years of power he was anxious to be rid were in general well-born and often had privileged access to the court.

Fortunately for him, Fisher made a favourable impression on Queen Victoria and, even more valuably, became an intimate friend of King Edward VII and Queen Alexandra. The Admiral's irrepressible high spirits, his love of life, his sense of fun, particularly endeared him to the King who at once recognized his remarkable gifts and his evident mastery of his profession. Without the support of the King and that of his shrewd and well-informed aides, Lord Knollys and Lord Esher, it is very doubtful whether Fisher would have been able to put through the revolutionary programme on which he embarked as First Sea Lord in October 1904 and which he had pretty well completed by the time he was forced to relinquish office early in 1910 as a result of the personal animosities between himself and the Commander-in-Chief of the Channel Fleet, Admiral Lord Charles Beresford.* He was certainly well seconded by his political chiefs, notably Lord Selborne who was First Lord in the Tory administration and Reginald McKenna who succeeded the rather vacuous Lord Tweedmouth in the great Liberal administration that came in in 1905. And George Lambert, the Civil Lord in that ministry, became, and remained through every vicissitude, his liege man. But the forces ranged against him, not merely political but social and professional, were so formidable that he needed every ally he could find in politics and the press: and even then it was only the massive weight of King Edward VII that turned the scale.

Fisher's combative temper did not make things easy for his friends. One of his favourite quotations was the fine epitaph of one of Nelson's captains: 'Death found him fighting'. Death would have

---

*Beresford had annoyed Fisher by his independence of mind while serving as Commander-in-Chief Mediterranean. Fisher as First Sea Lord did all he could to prevent him being appointed to the Channel Fleet but was overruled by Tweedmouth, the First Lord, whom he never forgave. Beresford accepted the offer in August 1906 but did not hoist his flag until the following April. In the intervening months Fisher seized the opportunity of a demand for reduction in the naval estimates to create a new command, the Home Fleet, which at first was to consist of battleships held in reserve with skeleton crews but rapidly grew in strength and importance, mainly at the expense of the Channel command. Beresford was not the man to take this lying down. A running fight developed between the Admiralty and the Commander-in-Chief which grew into a public scandal. In the end a Cabinet committee headed by the Prime Minister had to put a stop to it.

had to take careful aim indeed to find Lord Fisher in any other posture. The head-on clash of opinion and personality was meat and drink to him. Painting only in primary colours he rejected with contempt the softer tones of conciliation and compromise. No wonder King Edward VII once had occasion to say to him: 'I am the only friend you have.' Fisher's reply 'Yes, sir, but you have backed the winner' sums up their amused and affectionate intimacy. To the King, Fisher's reckless, even wanton, antagonizing of powerful figures was irresponsible almost to the point of idiocy. '. . . King Edward said I was not [a man of the world] and never would be! – "that I had gone all round the world but I had never been in it." '[8]

The King's perception goes to the heart of Fisher's qualities. For all the Admiral's intellectual energy, his unquenchable zest for life, his fearlessness, his gusto, his intrigues, his vendettas, there was, strangely enough, an innocence, a simplicity, about him that was the root of his strengths and of his weaknesses. Calm, clear, rational analysis and comparison was, like sobriety of judgement, all but impossible for him. Consistency, the hard-won product of these modes of thinking, he habitually ridiculed as the emblem of mediocrity. Speed, dash, brilliance were the qualities he valued and himself exemplified. He seized on ideas and extrapolated them with the imagination of genius but his critical faculties were uncertain to the point of caprice. Exactly the same is true of his relations with colleagues and subordinates: at one moment they were giants, at the next pygmies. Lord Charles Beresford, A. K. Wilson, Prince Louis of Battenberg, even his particular and prize model of a twentieth-century admiral, Jellicoe, all underwent, to a greater or a lesser degree, these dramatic revaluations.

Beresford, it must be admitted, gave some grounds for such a revision of judgement. Like Fisher, with whom he was closely associated professionally, he had been brought up in the old sailing ship navy and perhaps retained rather more of the outlook of an eighteenth-century officer. He was certainly much better placed to succeed in such an environment than Fisher would have been, since he was an aristocrat and extremely rich. As a corollary of this he early became familiar with the court, serving in the Royal Yacht and attending the future King Edward VII as ADC on his visit to India. He thus enjoyed all the advantages that Fisher lacked and by virtue of them shared those that Fisher had succeeded in acquiring through professional distinction. A vivid and attractive personality, humorous, generous, high-spirited, he did not come behind Fisher in combativeness or in readiness to let his superior officers know that he did not think much of time-hallowed conceptions and methods. Besides advantages of birth and wealth and of his unusually close connections with the Royal Family (he had served as First Lieutenant to another of Queen Victoria's sons, the Duke of Edinburgh) he was also, intermittently, an MP. Most emphatically he was not the man to allow a tradition of loyalty and subordination to inhibit his public criticism of any shortcomings in the service that came within his field of vision. In addition to all this he was a well-known and popular figure, a daring rider to hounds and a conspicuous and flamboyant member of the most fashionable society. His conquests were said to be many, his chef enjoyed a high reputation and those who had had a back view of him in a state of nature carried away a vivid recollection of a tattooed scene of a hunt in full cry after a fox.

Beresford, like Fisher, distinguished himself in action at the bombardment of Alexandria in 1882. Both men showed their characteristic dash and initiative in the operations carried out by the Naval Brigade to restore order ashore. Fisher's use of an armoured train caught the imagination of the public, while Beresford, who served directly under him in the post of Provost Marshal and Chief of Police, won golden opinions, not least from his commanding officer who thought that he ought to have been included in the honours list. For the next quarter of a century they continued good friends, indeed rather as professional allies against the complacent conservatism that both saw as the enemy within the service. Fisher frequently praised Beresford's tactical skill in Fleet exercises. Beresford served as Fisher's second-in-command of the Mediterranean Fleet at the turn of the century. The quarrel that divided them and did such severe damage to the cohesion, the all-important mutual trust and loyalty of the whole naval profession, arose out of Fisher's reorganization of the Fleet dispositions against the growing threat from Germany when he was First Sea Lord and Beresford was Commander-in-Chief of the Channel Fleet.

The importance of the quarrel lay in its results, not its cause. Fisher, for all his intuitive response to the technological advances that were to revolutionize naval warfare, always tended to personalize issues of policy. And for all his radicalism, rather he would have maintained because of it, he was a whole-hearted élitist. 'Favouritism is the secret of efficiency', the words that he wrote in the log of HMS *Vernon*, was one of his favourite aphorisms, borrowed from Admiral Hope, under whom he had served as a young officer on the China Station. Favouritism, as Fisher understood it, was the answer to the inertia of letting the most important appointments decide themselves by reference to an officer's position in the Navy List. 'Going by seniority saves so much trouble. "*Buggins' turn*" has been our ruin and will be disastrous hereafter! Can we pass over Buggins is the question! What a fuss there will be!'⁹ The able officer without birth or money could only rise fast and far by catching the eye of a superior who would single him out, further his promotion and press his qualities on the men who were running the navy. This was how Fisher himself had been enabled to climb to a position from which he could influence the development of the service. This was what he meant by favouritism. It was not at all the same thing as nepotism. In Fisher's eyes it was indeed the antithesis of it.

All this meant that choosing the right men to train for the top jobs and bringing them on fast so that they were still young and energetic and ready to take risks, as Nelson had been when he first commanded a fleet, was the first duty of those politicians, administrators and sea officers to whose care the Navy had been entrusted. That again meant that Fisher, practising what he preached, was in close and regular correspondence with officers far junior to himself whom he treated as professional equals and whose opinions he invited on all manner of professional topics. Given his personal approach this led to his inviting, or at least appearing to invite, junior officers to criticize their seniors.

Thus came into existence what was known in the service as the 'Fishpond', a clientage of personal adherents on whom promotion would smile while those excluded were cast into outer darkness. It was this short-circuiting of discipline and subordination that at last gave Beresford the means of discomfiting him. Not that he had neglected any other. His position in society, his great private wealth were advantages that he well knew how to exploit. Above all, after the death of King Edward VII in 1910, Beresford had the ear of his successor, King George V, who had himself served as a naval officer. Fisher's resignation from the post of First Sea Lord took effect in January 1910, only a few months before the change of Sovereign, but he had been retained on the active list and encouraged to believe that he might shortly be recalled. It was to take a war and the full weight of Winston Churchill's influence as First Lord of the Admiralty and one of the most powerful members of Asquith's glittering administration to make this possible.

Fisher's personality is truly qualified by the epithet so often applied to it – 'magnetic' – since it exerted not only a powerful attraction but a no less strong repulsion. The Churchills, Winston and Clementine, provide a striking instance of a couple affected in diametrically opposite directions. That the feelings he excited divided the service he loved is incontestable. But it is hardly disputed that more than any single man he transformed the Royal Navy and, by doing so, sketched out the scenario for what he clearly saw from the start was an entirely new form of naval warfare. The letter already quoted in which he says that up to his time the strategy, tactics, ships and weapons of sea fighting had remained unchanged since the days of King Alfred is an exaggeration. The advent of gunnery in the age of the Tudors coincided with sudden advances in rigging and sail-plan to revolutionize naval warfare. The *Mary Rose* rising from her bed in the Solent has recently given tangible evidence of this. But though Fisher exaggerated he was in essence and in spirit right. What is more astonishing is that though in the successive technical advances of his own day he sometimes misjudged their consequences or significance, none the less in an awe-inspiring number of instances he hit the bull's-eye with his first shot. He was, in his talk and his letters, particularly fond of the analogy of the elephant's trunk which can be used to lift great trees in the teak forest or to pick up a safety-pin. His own vision had the same versatility.

Perhaps his greatest strength as an innovator was that he had proved his accomplishment in the old, fundamental arts of seamanship and gunnery. He remembered to the end of his life a homeward passage off the Cape of Good Hope in 1872 when HMS *Ocean*, one of the largest sailing vessels in the navy, was rolling so violently in such a tearing gale that her Captain, doubting if the men could be brought to go aloft unless the Commander led them in person, ordered Fisher to do so. Up on the fore-topmast yards his uniform jacket was torn in pieces by the force of the wind. Soon after his return he was appointed to HMS *Excellent*, Whale Island, the gunnery school at Portsmouth, then and for long after the naval holy of holies in the cult of the gun, where he used his arts of argument and persuasion to urge on his seniors the importance of the torpedo. So successful was he that he was instrumental in founding a complementary torpedo school, HMS *Vernon*. A few years later he was appointed Captain at Whale Island, for long one of the most coveted posts in the navy. He followed this up by becoming Director of Naval Ordnance, in which post he fought a long and entirely successful action with the government of the day to obtain naval control over the design and production of naval guns, hitherto vested in the War Office. Thus whatever ploys the fossils might use to frustrate the dangerous innovations that Fisher was every day pressing on the service they could not dismiss him as a jumped-up theoretician who did not know at first-hand the immemorial means of English naval supremacy.

What is especially remarkable about this blue-water sailor with his love for the Bible, his passion for the sermons of Jeremy Taylor, his instinctive feel for the genius of the English language, is his technical and mechanical understanding and enthusiasm. It was Fisher who brought the engineers into the wardroom as naval officers instead of keeping them at arm's length – and below the salt – as Inspectors of Machinery. More importantly he knew what they were talking about. Most important of all he could communicate his knowledge in vivid imagery and simple language so that politicians and civil servants could understand what was involved. Take for instance this passage from a letter to Lord Selborne, then First Lord of the Admiralty, explaining the advantages of the water-tube boiler whose adoption, against fierce opposition, Fisher pushed through. One argument used against it was that it had not been adopted by the leading ship-owners. Here is Fisher's rebuttal of one such critic:

He compares the Mercantile Marine with men-of-war. They don't admit of comparison. You can't compare a cabbage with a cheese! Just look at the conditions. In a man-of-war the engines have to be crammed under an armour deck below the waterline, and, horizontally, there are fighting conditions which cramp them also. But in the merchant steamer ample headroom is available, there are no limitations for the long stroke of piston, which is the secret of efficiency and sustained effort. Every schoolboy knows (as Lord Macaulay would have said) that the wear and tear of an engine does not depend so much upon the piston speed as upon the number of times the heaving moving parts of large and powerful engines have to be stopped and reversed in a given time, that is to say, *the number of revolutions in a minute*! It is this excess of reciprocating motion which causes the wear and tear of the engine in the man-of-war, with its short stroke, as compared with the unlimited conditions of the Mercantile Marine.

. . . All the above is in regard to the engines, but the boilers come under the same category. The tank boiler is a *mercantile* boiler. The water-tube boiler is a fighting boiler. There are fighting facilities afforded by the water-tube boiler which the tank boiler cannot give. You can't make a cheese have leaves like a cabbage! You can't get up steam if a few minutes in a tank boiler. You can't stop dead at your maximum speed in a tank boiler! You have got to the limit of the tank boiler.[10]

As a piece of expository prose this is a model. Every idea is crystal clear; the language matches the thought; the imagery is striking and immediately engages the reader's interest; above all the liveliness, the exuberance of the author's mind is perfectly reflected in the pace of his style. As a piece of advocacy it is formidable. Even in so short an extract so arbitrarily cut about it is easy to see how deep was the influence of another of his favourite aphorisms, 'Repetition is the soul of journalism'. This axiom, which he always attributed to Barnes, the great editor of *The Times*, surely applies with especial force to radical or crusading journalism. It is not surprising that Fisher, himself a radical who wished to transform opinion in his own field of activity, should learn from the techniques of the reforming propagandist. He in fact cultivated close relations with the leading radical editors and newspaper writers of his day, W. T. Stead, J. L. Garvin, C. P. Scott and A. G. Gardiner prominent among them. No service chief till Field Marshal Montgomery paid such attention to the press or took such pains to line up its support in advance. None of his predecessors had approached him in such endeavours and most would have stood aghast at the idea. Certainly his contemporaries looked down their noses. Perhaps for all the skill and charm with which he courted the media (what might he not have done if he had survived into the era of radio and television!) the effort was counter-productive. Disapproval of such activity ran so deep in the service and in the Court that he may have lost more than he gained. But it was wholly characteristic of him to have employed such methods and to have enjoyed outraging traditional sentiments by doing so.

Enjoyment was Fisher's secret weapon. After he had been forced into retirement as a result of the quarrel with Beresford he wrote to his wife: '. . . I enjoy every minute of the day every day I live, and am absolutely content and happy! . . .'[11] He had displayed the same quality as a junior officer when there was some tedious and exhausting task, such as coaling ship, to be undertaken. He enjoyed life on principle, however repellent its immediate aspect. This quality, rare as it is, is wonderfully infectious. As Dr Johnson long ago pointed out it is what makes Falstaff the most universally attractive of Shakespeare's creations. The moment he appears on the stage the spirits of the audience rise. So it was with Fisher whether he was turning out the watch below on a dirty night, addressing the junior officers of the Mediterranean Fleet on the principles of war, or lobbying politicians or courtiers on the virtues of the big gun. Of all his many gifts it was the most distinctive. Even Churchill who responded so deeply to it and to some extent shared it, paid for it by troughs of apathy and depression. Not until Fisher was a very old man and believed, with some reason, that his life's work was in ruins did his champagne-like gaiety show any signs of abating, and even then not much. For a profoundly serious man without a touch of flippancy about him it was a remarkable trait of character.

It was the first principle of Fisher's mind that it was able to eliminate, at once and totally, any counter-arguments or considerations to the proposition he was at the moment maintaining, even if they were those he had himself stated with no less cogency and conviction on some earlier occasion. His contempt for consistency might be disconcerting but it obviously lent him the speed and manoeuvrability that he so much prized in the warships whose design he superintended. One of his most conspicuous reversals of judgement was over Arthur Pollen's fire-control system which in its final development embodied the first electrically driven analog-computer. Its revolutionary feature was that it provided instant and automatic adjustment and correction of range while the firing ship and her target were both manoeuvring at speed. Accuracy of aim became for the first time a matter of technology.

This extraordinary story was first told by Pollen's son, Anthony, in his book *The Great Gunnery Scandal* (1980). It has since been documented beyond any possibility of doubt by Professor Jon Sumida in his Navy Records Society volume *The Pollen Papers* (1984) and further elucidated in his *In Defence of Naval Supremacy: Finance, Technology and British Naval Policy 1889–1914* (1989). Unfortunately, as Captain Roskill has pointed out, the Admiralty have destroyed the extensive correspondence engendered by this invention, originally welcomed by Fisher with characteristic vehemence and characteristic perception of its far-reaching potentialities: *'Pollen's invention is simply priceless*, and I do hope we may hesitate at nothing to get ITS SOLE USE. We shall NEVER be forgiven hereafter if we do not! . . . The case is marvellously like the introduction of the Whitehead torpedo. We could have had the absolute monopoly of that wonderful weapon (and Mr Whitehead body and soul into the bargain), but the Admiralty of that day haggled over £80,000 . . . I hope we shan't make such an idiotic mistake over Pollen!'[12] But they did, and Fisher, in the end, went along with them.

Why did so ardent a champion of technological innovation, so bold a prophet of future development in warfare repudiate his original insight? Pollen's invention was all that he said it was. It was at once adopted by every navy that could obtain it and, after the Fisher period, incorporated into the gunnery control system of the Royal Navy. In 1925 the Royal Commission on Awards to Inventors bestowed its belated but financially convincing recognition on it. Is it out of character that the man who, against the world, proclaimed the revolutionary importance of the submarine, the aircraft, the turbine, oil fuel, wireless telegraphy and every other significant development affecting the nature of sea warfare, should have gone back on his own judgement? It is not the inconsistency that calls for explanation. It is that having hit the bull's-eye first time he should then insist that he had missed the target.

In the absence of the papers destroyed by those charged with sifting the Admiralty records this problem can never be conclusively solved. But there are some indications as to the likely chain of cause and effect. Fisher's extraordinary entrepreneurial flair, his power of penetrating at once to the heart of the matter, was not matched by an equal sureness of judgement when it came to people. His opinions were no less categoric but the instinct that formed them was by no means so astonishing. It is true that he picked and backed some classic winners. Hankey had caught his eye as an unusually intelligent and active-minded young Marine officer during the time that he was commanding the Mediterranean Fleet. But Hankey was bound to have caught someone's eye. Indeed Fisher's enemy-to-be, Lord Charles Beresford, had already recognized his potentialities as an intelligence officer and had appointed him to his staff. None the less, Fisher must take the lion's share of the credit for helping Hankey up the ladder that led him, fortunately for his country, to the Secretaryship of the Cabinet and of the Committee of Imperial Defence during the First World War.

Of others that Fisher could claim as his particular protégés Jellicoe is manifestly the most famous. But two of the leading, perhaps indeed *the* leading, naval thinkers and writers of the first half of the twentieth century, Admiral Sir Herbert Richmond and the historian Sir Julian Corbett owed much to his encouragement and were proud to own themselves his disciples.

These names are impressive enough; but they are chosen because their achievement and reputation are known well beyond the circle of professional officers. To evaluate Fisher's contribution to the service by bringing on men who did stout work in their day but are now known only to specialists would try the reader's patience. It would do so unnecessarily because all that requires to be established is that Fisher can take credit for having championed some of the most valuable of those who succeeded him as leaders of the service and as protagonists, informed and informing, of naval opinion. By the same token it must also be made clear that he consistently disparaged and did his best to obstruct some other officers who can certainly claim to have rendered outstanding service. Admiral Sir Reginald 'Blinker' Hall, the brilliant intelligence officer, is never mentioned in Fisher's correspondence without a sneer. Yet he gathered round him in Room 40 at the Admiralty the nucleus of cryptographers whose reading of enemy signals could, properly handled, have changed the course of the war. Bletchley Park, the centre of such activity in the Second World War, derived directly from Hall's organization. Indeed some of the people in charge of Bletchley had been picked by Hall 25 years earlier. Admiral of the Fleet Sir Roger Keyes is another far from negligible officer who incurred Fisher's deepest scorn. Even Beatty who is sometimes allowed to have some professional merit is more often damned with grudging praise.

Thus among those whose services posterity has agreed to be eminent Fisher has his hits and his misses. And as to the misses it is difficult not to feel that personal animosity rather than detached professional judgement is sometimes the principal cause. Fisher was in so many important respects so truly magnanimous – he set no store by titles, he laughed at decorations and full-dress uniforms, he never fell for the deceitfulness of riches (and his lack of money was often irksome since he was both generous and hospitable) – that it seems censorious to single out his shortcomings. But he himself was too serious a Christian and too amused an observer of his own personality to be entirely unaware of them. 'I may have to be egotistical', he wrote to Lord Rosebery in July 1917, adding in parentheses 'I've come to the conclusion that it's only a d—d fool or a saint who is not egotistical, and I don't claim to be either!'[13] Egotism certainly suggests itself as the probable explanation of Fisher's aberrations in judgement of people. His concern for his own opinion occluded his natural gifts of intelligence and openness of mind.

It is not simply that he misjudged or underrated people who proved themselves to be of undeniable quality. It is much more that he exaggerated, often to an absurd degree, the abilities of those who reflected his own burning enthusiasms or at least for the time appeared to do so. Two officers in particular, Admiral of the Fleet Sir Arthur Wilson and Admiral Sir Frederic Dreyer, come to mind in connection with the Pollen affair. Wilson, who was to succeed

Fisher as First Sea Lord in 1910, enjoyed a reputation in the service as a tactician and as a Fleet Commander. He was Fisher's junior by a year and their careers offer obvious comparisons. Wilson took part in the action against the Peiho forts, he distinguished himself at the bombardment of Alexandria and in the subsequent excitements over the armoured train, he took a leading part in the development of the torpedo and received, time and again, the highest encomiums from his more articulate and expansive contemporary. 'He was the man', wrote Fisher in his *Memories*, 'so head-and-shoulders above all his fellows, who in his time was our undoubted, indeed our incomparable, Sea Leader. No one touched him.'[14] He was also the man who rejected Pollen's invention in terms which were both arrogant and abusive.[15] Unlike Fisher, Wilson was not a happy or successful representative of the service in its public or political relations. At the crucial meeting of the Committee of Imperial Defence called by Asquith in August 1911 to consider what Britain should do if she became involved in the European war that the Germans seemed to be threatening over the Agadir crisis, Wilson put up a performance that appalled so judicious and instructed a defender of maritime strategy as Hankey. Winston Churchill, who was also present though not yet First Lord of the Admiralty, was deeply disturbed at what seemed to him an exhibition of pure incompetence. The result, incidentally, was that the superior presentation of the War Office carried all before it and committed the country to the policy, anathema to Fisher, of a full-scale land war on the Continent, pre-empting at a stroke all the options that the leading sea-power had open to her.[16]

Admiral Sir Frederic Dreyer, some 35 years younger than Fisher and Wilson, was the rising star among the gunnery officers of the new generation. It was his success as gunnery officer of the *Exmouth*, Wilson's flagship, that drew him into the inner circle where Fisher and Wilson planned the remodelling of the navy. Naturally he was deeply involved in the testing and reporting on Pollen's instruments of fire-control. Unfortunately he was also, or at any rate was accepted as, a rival inventor. Whether or not he plagiarized some of Pollen's work, as has been suggested, there can be no question that it was highly improper for him to act in the dual role of competitor and judge. That he was enabled to do so is the clear responsibility of Wilson and Fisher. And in the last resort this is attributable to Fisher's grotesquely exaggerated estimate of his capacities. Dreyer 'has the brain of a Newton' he had written in 1908.[17]

The flaw in Fisher's mentality was his contempt for system. The brilliance of his intuition led him to despise the rational plodding of analysis, criticism and comparison when he suspected that these might lead to undesired conclusions. His uncharacteristic failure to seize and exploit the incalculable advantage of the Pollen system may thus be ascribed to his excessive confidence in his own judgement of people. This is proverbially one of the commonest manifestations of egotism to which he cheerfully pleaded guilty.

> To Observations which ourselves we make
> We grow more partial for th' Observer's sake.

It is equally probable that his blindness to the brilliant work of Room 40 was caused by his dislike of Admiral Hall. For qualities so prodigious as Fisher's a price must be paid.

After all, nearly every other admiral of his time would have fallen into his errors. As a matter of historical fact most of them did. What none of them came near was the range and multiplicity of his vision or the flexibility, the readiness to respond to new ideas or to changed circumstances which age could not wither. Indeed in many respects, certainly in his views of politics and society, he grew more radical as he grew older. He had always despised the class system and laughed at snobbery. In his later age, embittered by what he believed to be King George V's partiality towards Beresford and convinced that Court influence was obstructing his own re-employment in the higher direction of the war, he even permitted himself in one of his letters (printed but not remarked by Professor Marder) the disrespect of the ribald nickname by which the King and his consort were known: futile George and fertile Mary.[18] Such language, even in a private letter, from an Admiral of the Fleet who had been principal naval ADC to the preceding monarch is strong stuff. It echoes the note, periodically recurrent in his view of the two armed services of his day, '. . . ever since Cromwell it has always been *"the People's Navy"* and *"the Court Army"*. . .'[19] Fisher's grasp of history was uncertain. After Nelson his two great heroes were Napoleon and Cromwell. But it is strange that he credits Cromwell with the ethos and achievements of the Commonwealth navy and never so much as mentions the admiral whom even Nelson regarded as his superior – 'I do not reckon myself equal to Blake'. Probably the historical approach, the weighing of evidence, the attempt to understand what people very different from oneself were after and why, was thoroughly uncongenial to him. It was the kind of mumbling, shuffling occupation fit for Buggins or Stiggins. Much better thrust your hand boldly into the bran tub of the past and use whatever fact you came up with to shy at some old fossil who was blocking your way.

This belief in the inspiration of the moment, this reliance on intellectual shooting from the hip, is all very well for someone equipped with Fisher's extraordinary brilliance and penetration. But if he had been an historian and not a naval officer he would have found that it was not enough. The much-derided labours of Buggins and Stiggins would have to be called in at some stage if scholarly criticism were to be met and properly founded objections satisfied. Was it in fact enough even as a naval officer? Was not Fisher's steady objection to the creation of a proper naval staff, to examine, to analyse, to classify, to prepare and to record, rooted in the arrogant impatience of a man who knew himself to be faster and better-armed than any opponent who might challenge him? Perhaps it was intensified by the fact that Beresford had, improbably enough, been a consistent advocate of the measure. Predictably, Sir Arthur Wilson had been violently opposed to it. Yet Hankey, who was unstinting in his admiration for Fisher and enjoyed his good opinion from first to last, was untiring in his efforts to set up such an organization. Only in the last year of the war was he successful. To this delay may be attributed the chief blame for the mismanagement of naval affairs, most notably the failure to develop measures against the U-boats that all but brought the country to its knees.

Perhaps the most remarkable tribute to Fisher's standing in the eyes of politicians and administrators was his appointment while he was Commander-in-Chief at Portsmouth to a committee consisting only of himself, Lord Esher and Sir George Clarke,* to reorganize the War Office. This immediately preceded his appointment to the post of First Sea Lord in October 1904. To be invited to reform the central organ of policy and administration in a sister service is a rare honour, indeed for an admiral in the Royal Navy a unique one. One of the results of the Committee's report was the creation of an Army General Staff. Why, it may be asked, did Fisher recommend for the army what he opposed for the navy? He would have replied that the nature of generalship was altogether different from that of admiralty; that no general, who was not insane, would be in the thick of the battle where communication was impossible and changes in tactical disposition correspondingly so. A good general would be well behind the line where supported by his staff he would receive information and issue the necessary orders. The admiral, on the other hand, must be on the scene, able to observe and to react in a split second, which the conditions of sea-fighting permitted him to do. Dominating all was Fisher's conception of a sea officer whose senses and instincts had been sharpened to so fine a point that action was a reflex, not the product of cogitation, almost like a wild animal whose survival depends on speed of reaction to phenomena, not on rational analysis of them. People who work on staffs, he argued, are essentially clerks, administrators, civil servants. The naval officer is not trained to be a clerk, and does not make a good one.

There can be no doubt that Fisher believed this. What is more open to question is whether he had ever thought his position through or considered it in relation to his own practice. Few men

*Later Lord Sydenham of Combe, Secretary Colonial Defence Committee 1885–1892 and of Committee of Imperial Defence 1904–7.

can have been more extrovert than he (at least in his maturity: there are signs that in his time as a midshipman and a young lieutenant he looked at himself long and hard). Yet can he have really remained ignorant of how much his own successes depended on rigorous, sustained intellectual analysis? He exults in old age over the reform programme he put through in his years as First Sea Lord from 1904 to 1910: '. . . those glorious reforming years in which we got rid of $19\frac{1}{2}$ millions sterling of parasites, and reduced the age of our Admirals . . . and got it realized that engines and not sails produced the better man.'[20] Could he possibly have argued that that enormous and complicated programme came to him as he walked through the screen of the Admiralty courtyard in October 1904? On the contrary he makes it clear that he had used his time as Commander-in-Chief Portsmouth to work out in detail what he would do if, as seemed highly probable, he succeeded to the position of First Sea Lord. Or take for example a letter he wrote to Asquith in March 1916, when he was out of office but had been asked to attend a meeting of the War Council at which Admiralty construction policy had been discussed. Fisher was then 75; he had no secretariat; yet he produced a memorandum (for that is in effect what the letter is) on the broad questions and on important points of detail running to some 3,000 words of which not one is otiose. The sweep, the force, of the document demands reproduction in its entirety. But even quotation by sample shows a power of mind that comes from discipline, from system, from practice, not from mere rapidity of reflex.

It is an entirely fallacious statement that delay in the delivery of one vessel is any reason why others should not be ordered at the same time in the same yard. The men who finish a ship do not do the early work on her, and so long as the vessel is launched and the slip vacant, another vessel can be commenced with little or no interference; there is no reason whatever why succeeding vessels should also be late. It is not surprising that there will be a shortage if these principles have been followed.

I was always being told at the Admiralty that things could not possibly be done. But they were done! The same arguments appear to hold the field again. I was informed that the *Invincible* could not leave Devonport [to attack von Spee's squadron] for two days after the day appointed, because of some defect in the brickwork of her boilers. But she went, and I have not heard since of any ill result! Had those two days been lost, von Spee would have been missed by two days at the Falkland Islands and many things would have been changed. I was told on arriving at the Admiralty and finding that no new submarines had then been ordered since the war broke out, that it was impossible for anybody but Vickers to make the engines, and that for this reason and for many others the possible output was very limited. Nevertheless, within a few days large orders were placed with many shipbuilders who had never built submarines or engines before, and I am informed that these are being delivered and are quite satisfactory. I was told that the monitors could not be built in time, and I could cite many examples where the so-called impossible was achieved.[21]

Whatever Fisher might say in exuberant contempt of mediocrity and conventional wisdom he could not have achieved what he did without applying the steady, sober, rational habit of mind at which he was always girding. From time to time he admits as much. 'I fully agree with you about the Navy want of first-class intellects. Concentration and discipline combine to cramp the Sea Officer . . . Great views don't get grasped,'[22] he wrote to Esher in January 1912. The context of the letter lends weight to the judgement. It was written from Naples whither Fisher, ever a lover of sun and warmth, had retired after he had been relieved as First Sea Lord in 1910. Soon after his departure Winston Churchill who had long thirsted for the Admiralty succeeded Reginald McKenna as First Lord. No doubt if Churchill had had a free hand he would have recalled Fisher then and there, since as has been mentioned he had already formed the lowest opinion of his successor, Sir Arthur

Wilson. To do so would have presented grave difficulties; Fisher's age for one thing, his quarrelsomeness for another and, above all, after the change of reign the strong disapproval of King George V who took a personal interest in the affairs of his old service. What happened therefore was that Churchill conducted an extensive and highly secret correspondence with his old friend, asking his advice on appointments, inviting his suggestions on all manner of questions from ship construction and weapons to improving the conditions and prospects of the lower deck, in short treating him as his principal professional adviser.

It is remarkable that this relationship should have remained unknown to the press and the public during the two and a half years that passed before Fisher was eventually induced to return to England in an official capacity to take the Chair of the Royal Commission on Oil Fuel and Oil Engines for the Royal Navy, the culmination of one of his most far-reaching policies of modernization. It is even more remarkable that the Sea Lords on Churchill's Board of Admiralty, old friends and colleagues of Fisher's whose feelings and position he took care to respect, should not have realized what was going on. But what was most remarkable of all was that two such tornadoes as Churchill and Fisher should have swept across the oceans of naval policy and organization without violent collision. Only once, in the spring of 1912, did Fisher break off relations when he considered that Churchill had surrendered two key positions to the Court, by consenting to Beresford's promotion to Admiral of the Fleet and by appointing three admirals favoured by the King but despised by Fisher to important commands. What was particularly serious was that it appeared to secure the succession of one of them to the position of First Sea Lord and to risk one of the others obtaining the chief sea command in the event of war, an appointment that Fisher and Churchill had previously agreed should go to Jellicoe. '. . . I fear this must be my last communication with you in any matter at all. I am sorry for it, but I consider you have betrayed the navy in these three appointments . . . I am going to transfer my body and my money to the United States – I can't remedy what has been done – and it's no d—d use squealing . . . Adieu.'[23]

No doubt Fisher's emotions had been excited by Wilson's replacement as First Sea Lord earlier in the year. It was apropos this that he wrote the letter to Esher already quoted about the intellectual poverty of the navy. Prince Louis of Battenberg, Wilson's successor, had earlier been characterized by Fisher as one of the two best officers in the navy but now he was dismissed as 'only a superior sort of *commis voyageur*'. His friend Lord Esher was even less flattering: 'The man is just above the average, and that is all.'[24] It would have been a renunciation of the world impossible for a man of Fisher's temperament if he had not been tantalized by the thought of being recalled to the post himself.

The breach, far from being final, was soon bridged. A bare fortnight later he was writing to his son '. . . Well! as regards Winston Churchill "amantium irae amoris integratio est" [the quarrels of lovers knit them even closer] . . .', adding, however, later in the letter '. . . I am not so cordial towards Winston as I was, nor shall I ever be again.'[25] How far Churchill had gone to placate him is evident on every hand, not least from this same letter: '. . . he really has replied very nicely that no matter what I like to say to him, he is going to stick to me and support all my schemes and always maintain that I am a genius and the greatest naval administrator, etc., etc., etc.' Only a few months later Fisher returned at the pressing invitation of both Churchill and the Prime Minister to head the Royal Commission. As a result of its report the Government acquired in August 1914 a majority shareholding in what then became the Anglo–Persian Oil Company. Not since Holland in the seventeenth century had made herself the greatest sea power in the world without having within her frontiers any of the essentials for building or propelling ships had so bold a gamble been taken by a first-class naval power. But if ever a man lived up to his own maxims it was Fisher. He never tired of preaching that 'Boldness in war is Prudence and Prudence Imbecility'. Or as he put it more picturesquely in a letter to C. P. Scott (of all people!): '. . . The element of success in war is SURPRISE. To beget SURPRISE you must arrange for IMAGINATION to go to bed with AUDACITY.'[26]

It had been long understood that in the event of war Fisher would put his services at his country's disposal. In the summer of 1914 he abandoned his usual visit to Marienbad. His daughter and son-in-law had been less circumspect and were interned on the outbreak of war. A great part of Fisher's energies in the first few weeks of hostilities was employed in securing their release. In October the authorities agreed to deport them to Italy where the Admiral, finding that little use was made of his presence in London, was planning to join them. However, the mishandling of the opening moves of the war at sea, most notably in the Mediterranean where the *Goeben* and the *Breslau* evaded superior forces to reach the security of the Dardanelles, thus bringing decisive pressure to bear on Germany's wavering ally Turkey, provoked a public outcry. Prince Louis of Battenberg, as First Sea Lord, was the obvious target, though in fact most historians would now agree that the blame should be divided between the imprecise instructions drafted by Churchill and the somewhat wooden interpretation of them by the Commander-in-Chief in the Mediterranean. Battenberg's German origins unfortunately provided the cheap press with an all too easy means of whipping up nationalist hysteria. On 30 October he resigned and Churchill seized the chance of bringing back Fisher.

When the country went to war it seemed, broadly, that everything modern or hopeful in the navy derived from Fisher. In fact at the Fleet Review that immediately preceded hostilities one of the younger admirals who was no protégé of his is on record as saying just this. That the man who had forged this unrivalled weapon should be given the opportunity to wield it in a war that he had long foreseen and whose outbreak he had predicted, month and year, to Hankey some four years earlier was surely one of the rare meetings and matchings of men and events. That he should be supported with devoted admiration and loyalty by one of the greatest war ministers in our history seemed unimaginable good fortune. Yet eight months later both men were politically and professionally ruined and each had good reason to blame the other.

What went wrong? The short answer, very short, only two words, is 'The Dardanelles'. That is a story too well-known, too often told, particularly by Churchill and his champions, to need rehearsal here. What is crucial to any understanding of the Admiral's personality is to disentangle the questions of patriotic duty, professional ethics, and personal loyalty involved in it. In short to present the moral issues as he saw them. For Fisher, for all the cynicism and mischief of his wit, for all the exaggerations and perversities and caprices of one who knew himself to be a star performer, was a moral man. 'Do right, and d—n the odds', the favourite of his many favourite maxims, was the true compass card by which he steered. His determination that the Devil should not have all the best tunes, or all the best jokes, has sometimes obscured this.

He was well aware that he would not have been recalled without Churchill's staking his own career on the choice. That, combined with deep sympathy and long friendship, formed a strong loyalty, almost, to outward appearances, an indissoluble bond. It was at once reinforced by the brilliant success with which this partnership opened. Fisher was perfectly entitled to claim, as he did in the letter to Asquith already quoted, that without his instant assessment of the situation and lightning promptitude in hustling out the battle cruisers against the protests of the responsible authorities the victory over von Spee would not have been won. And Churchill who would have had to take the blame if Fisher had made a mess of things was equally entitled to take credit for so resounding and so timely a reassertion of British sea-power.

Thus when a few weeks later Churchill nailed his colours to the mast of the Dardanelles, Fisher was caught in a conflict of professional and personal and patriotic loyalties. In the first place, like Hankey and other experts, he thought the concept a fruitful one if it was in support of a landing force. As it became clearer that a purely naval attempt on the Straits was intended, his opposition

47

hardened. His alarm at Churchill's readiness to risk even the new *Queen Elizabeth* battleships for such uncertain gains drove him frantic. Without the *Queen Elizabeths* the Grand Fleet lost its margin over the German High Seas Fleet. Nothing less than the command of the sea was at stake. No responsible First Sea Lord could allow a Government to embark on such a policy without forcing it to recognize exactly what it was doing. As early as 28 January 1915 – that is to say within a fortnight of Churchill's plan being approved by the War Council – Fisher had determined that resignation was his only course. He attended the War Council meeting on that day, resolved to announce his decision but was persuaded to hold his hand after a private conversation with Lord Kitchener who rose from the Council table and drew him aside. What did Kitchener say? Information derived from the Fisher family – the Admiral left no record of the conversation – suggests that he laid particular stress on the Allied negotiations with Italy, a much courted neutral who joined the Allies some four months later. Fisher's resignation over the conduct of the war was bound to produce a crisis of confidence at home and abroad. Such an appeal to his patriotism from such a source could have but one result. None the less he made no secret of his misgivings. 'The Dardanelles is futile without soldiers,' he wrote to Lloyd George on 23 February.[27]

Lloyd George in his *Memoirs* makes Fisher's view of his own obligations plain. Meeting him by chance at the entrance to 10 Downing Street on the morning of his resignation on 15 May he taxed him with having kept silent at meetings of the War Council when the Dardanelles expedition was discussed. '. . . it was only right that we should be given an opportunity of hearing his objections, weighing his advice, and taking the appropriate action. His answer was that Mr Churchill was his Chief, and that by the traditions of the service he was not entitled to differ from him in public.'[28] The postponement of the resignation had only made it more explosive in its effects. The continued strain of unwilling condonation of a policy he believed to be wrong in conception and perilous in execution had upset the balance of a mind never characterized by sobriety. Churchill's impropriety of conduct in issuing actual operational instructions, a function that undoubtedly belonged to the professional officers headed by the Sea Lords, drove Fisher to act with a wildness that made his return to office unthinkable. He resigned, as Lloyd George pointed out to him, without giving the competent authorities any opportunity of hearing his reasons or taking account of his professional recommendations. He left his letter of resignation with the Prime Minister, refused to see him, announced that he was going to Scotland and disappeared from the Admiralty and from his London house. Asquith was naturally infuriated. The resignation, together with the newspaper revelations of an inadequate supply of high-explosive shell, had made a reconstruction of the Government inevitable. There were indications that the German High Seas fleet might be coming out. It was insufferable that the First Sea Lord should at such a moment, on his own whim, vanish into thin air. Fisher was found to be lurking in the Charing Cross Hotel and was ordered on the King's authority to return to his post.

In his conversations with the Prime Minister, the Foreign Secretary and others, Fisher quickly realized that the Government had sustained a profound shock. He had, as he always did, been keeping in close touch with his Fleet Street friends, no doubt calculating that if his resignation was to have the desired effect of reversing the Dardanelles policy, a newspaper campaign was an essential reinforcement. In fact the coincidence of the so-called Shell Scandal had already forced Asquith to abandon a purely Liberal administration and to throw over Haldane, his oldest political friend, as part of the price of Conservative support. But the most important part of that price, from Fisher's point of view, was the insistence of the Conservatives that Churchill must leave the Admiralty. It thus seemed to him that he had got the Prime Minister in a corner and that he could dictate his own terms. This, in a letter that no head of government could conceivably accept, he at once proceeded to do. The tone and content were so altogether unreasonable that even its writer soon came to see that he should never have sent it. His staunchest champions from his official biographer, Admiral Bacon, to the most skilful restorer of his fame, the late Professor Arthur Marder, have found nothing to say for it. It played straight into the hands of his enemies. The Prime Minister wrote him a curt one-line letter of dismissal. The King was more courteous but notably cool. For all his unrivalled gifts, his knowledge, his insight, his astonishing achievements Fisher was finished.

He was not the man to accept this. And strangely enough neither was Winston Churchill. Kept out of any active responsibility for the conduct of the war by the bitter distrust of the Conservative leaders he had resigned his sinecure Cabinet post in November 1915 and had served for some months in the trenches. In March 1916 he came back on leave and rose from the back benches to speak on the Naval Estimates. In measured terms he voiced the disquiet that was so widely felt in informed circles, not least by Jellicoe, about the passivity of the Admiralty under Balfour and Sir Henry Jackson. In a hushed and deeply anxious House he reached his peroration:

> No personal consideration must stand between the country and those who can serve her best. I feel that there is in the present Admiralty administration, for all their competence, loyalty and zeal, a lack of driving force and mental energy which cannot be allowed to continue, which must be rectified while time remains and before evil results, and can only be rectified in one way. I am sure the nation and the Navy expect that the necessary step will be taken . . . I urge the First Lord of the Admiralty without delay to fortify himself, to vitalize and animate his Board of Admiralty by recalling Lord Fisher to his post as First Sea Lord . . .

Lady Violet Bonham Carter who prints this passage in her portrait, lit by a lifetime's affection and admiration, *Winston Churchill as I Knew Him*, recalls her own horrified reaction as she heard the speech: 'Had I gone mad? Had Winston?' It was, after all, her father's administration against which the gravamen lay. And no one can have known better than Churchill that if Fisher *were* brought back the Prime Minister could not have retained a shred of credibility or authority. It was, of course, easy for Arthur Balfour to quote Churchill's earlier opinions of Fisher's conduct over the Dardanelles. Easy, and devastating in debate. Churchill must have foreseen that. But that he was none the less prepared to call for Fisher's return, old, quarrelsome, devious and vindictive as even his admirers admitted him to be, is perhaps the greatest tribute ever paid to his genius and achievements.

Fisher lived on till 1920. As long as the war threatened the country with disaster, which it did almost to the very end, he never gave up hope of re-employment or abandoned his plots and machinations to that end. In public he preserved a dignified silence, confident that his reputation would be vindicated and contemptuous of those who put such considerations above the need to present a united front to the enemy. His counsel was sought from time to time by the politicians, officials and commanders who were running the war but on the whole he was left to chair a distinguished but impotent Committee on Invention and Research and to conduct the correspondence which has left so lively a reflection of his character.

Of his achievements and of his personal impact on the development of navies and sea-fighting in the twentieth century, one might almost repeat the epitaph of Sir Christopher Wren under the dome of St Paul's: 'Si monumentum requiris, circumspice'. In 1982, the creator of the huge Soviet Navy, Admiral Gorshkov, launched yet another vast submarine with the tonnage of a battleship, recalling irresistibly the submersible battlecruisers for which Fisher was clamouring towards the end of his career. In 1912 Fisher wrote to Churchill from Naples on this very subject, predicting that battle tactics would be revolutionized – and he ended with the words 'hurry up aviation'.[29] It would be tedious further to multiply examples even though a voice from the shades insists that 'repetition is the soul of journalism'.

The Royal Navy will forget her cunning when she forgets him.

But of all extraordinary, not to say bizarre, figures to have reached such eminence in that service Fisher surely leads the field. He was everything the navy of his time wasn't. He was irreverent, witty, openly deriding rank and age and protocol. He preached and not infrequently practised insubordination. He was a natural radical and was not really sound on the monarchy, devoted though he was to King Edward and Queen Alexandra. The range of his insights and of his curiosity, the astonishingly accurate prophecies both about the likely course of events and about the wider potentialities of weapons that had hardly been invented, much less developed, are matched by judgements on politics and history and the character of nations so childish in their naivety that one sometimes wonders if he had any centre of gravity at all. Perhaps he had only a centre of hilarity. Certainly he could not bear either boring or being bored. His draft reply to a Parliamentary question as to whether his new scheme for training officers was a success and if so, why it had not been introduced earlier: 'The answer to the first part is in the affirmative, as regards the second part it might have been asked the Deity as regards the Creation'[30] has the touch of Dean Swift. And Swift perhaps was his model when he startled the delegates to the Hague Peace Conference in 1899 by his suggestion that prisoners taken from enemy submarines should be boiled in oil. It was not to be taken literally: but he thought it important to emphasize to that well-intentioned gathering that war cannot be made anything but terrifying and horrible.

The journalists and politicians with whom he found himself in immediate sympathy were nearly all radicals: W. T. Stead, C. P. Scott, Sir Charles Dilke ('He is the one man in the House of Commons who is invariably right on naval affairs . . . [a] great political authority.'[31]) and many others already mentioned. He was immediately attracted to Garibaldi. On the one occasion on which he met Mr Gladstone at a dinner party the Grand Old Man was so taken with his company that he preferred to walk home with him instead of taking the brougham his wife had waiting at the door.[32] His ordinary talk, his lectures, his speeches, his official memoranda, his private correspondence by the general agreement of all who heard or read them could never for a moment be dull. He was, in the clumsy but expressive phrase of our day, a compulsive communicator.

It is difficult not to feel that this was the real root of his genius. He could not let an idea stagnate. He must launch it on the current of the world and, in his mind's eye, watch it turn and twist, revealing new aspects at each angle of vision. Suppose that he had never entered the navy, that he had become an engineer, a chemist, an imperial administrator, a civil servant or a journalist, it seems on the face of it probable that he would have left a famous name to posterity. Essentially he was an infant prodigy who never acquired the maturity of the grown-up or lost the zest of boyhood. And yet when he was required to 'Be of good cheer and play the man' he answered the call. There is no end to the contradictions of Jacky Fisher and to misquote one of his favourite apothegms '*La génie a ses raisons que la raison ne connaît point*'.

CUNNINGHAM

SOME of the contrasts between Cunningham and Fisher have already been suggested. Certainly their upbringing and education were as different as possible. Fisher's parents living like frontiersmen in the wild highlands of Ceylon before roads and tea-estates had tamed them seem to have taken hardly more interest in their numerous offspring than did the wild animals that surrounded them. Jacky was packed off to England at the age of six and thereafter was barely in touch with his father and mother. Andrew Cunningham's father was Professor of Anatomy first at Dublin and then at Edinburgh. Although his son records that his father's working hours – he left home at 7.30 and on his return worked in his study till after midnight – left little time for them to enjoy each other's company, they were clearly on amiable if somewhat remote terms. His mother supplied and received the ardent affection that is the life of childhood. The whole family was, one gathers, happy, close-knit and high-minded without being priggish or holier than thou. An academic background meant that education and an awareness of the life of the mind were accepted as a matter of course though in A. B. Cunningham's case without enthusiasm. As a schoolboy he 'could not abide Latin, French and English and was quite useless at them.' Mathematics came easily to him and throughout his life he never experienced any difficulty in passing examinations. As he grew older, he impressed his colleagues and superiors with his obvious powers of mind. Yet his tastes remained as markedly averse to the intellectual and the literary as they had been at the outset.

Cunningham says of himself that he had always been lazy. The demonic energy that he exemplified and demanded throughout his long career in the Service suggests that what he meant was that he felt no impulse of disinterested intellectual curiosity. The powerful machinery of which he felt himself master needed a practical motive to set it going. No doubt this might have been supplied if like other indolent but able boys he had been stimulated by brilliant teaching or jostled by competition. Perhaps this would have happened if he had stayed on at Edinburgh Academy. But, when his father telegraphed from Dublin 'Would you like to go into the navy?' and the ten-year-old replied 'Yes, I should like to be an admiral', that put paid to that. Three years at a naval crammer at Fareham were followed in 1897 by a cadetship.

Whether or not the great Duke of Wellington ever said that the Battle of Waterloo was won on the playing-fields of Eton has been disputed. But if he did say it what is indisputable is that he was not paying tribute to the team spirit which organized games-playing has been supposed to foster. Organized games did not exist at Eton at that period. What the playing-fields were famous for were the private fights between boys which were then thought to be the foundation of manliness. A hundred years after Dr Keate the same tradition was honoured in the training-ship *Britannia*. Cunningham recalls little of his education there but his contemporaries, among them Admiral of the Fleet Sir James Somerville who was to share so many of the same hazards in the Second World War, vividly recollect his pugnacity. Cunningham's nickname 'Meatface' and his characteristic reaction 'Fight you on Sunday' – the day on which the cadets were allowed a few brief hours of unsupervised solitude – survived in memory when everything else about his time at Dartmouth had been forgotten. He passed out respectably but inconspicuously and was sent, at his own request, to do his seatime on the South African station.

Taking passage out in a liner he beat Cecil Rhodes in the final of the ship's chess championship. The fact is made the more remarkable by Cunningham himself having recorded it in his autobiography. His horror of showing-off would hardly have allowed him to report a success in anything more serious than a game of deck quoits. It is the first glint of gold.

Two years' midshipman's-time on the South African station seem to have been sharply divided between the easy-going, enjoyable, uncrowded life abroad the light cruiser *Fox* and time spent in the heavy cruiser that was flagship of the squadron. Not only was she hideously overcrowded but the messing was inadequate: it was 'a generally unhappy time . . . we suffered from unpleasant sub-lieutenants'. Quite how vile a life of bullying and humiliation may be covered by this it is impossible to say. But such expressions from so granite a personality suggest that things must have been pretty bad. Charles Morgan's *The Gun Room* gives a first-hand description of what might have been met with ten years later and it does not make pleasant reading.

Nothing could have been more opportune therefore than the outbreak of the Boer War. Field Marshal Lord Roberts was a friend of the Cunningham family – so far as can be seen their only influential connection in the army or the navy. But it was through the Major of Marines aboard the cruiser being sent to replace another officer killed in action with the Naval Brigade that the sixteen-year-old midshipman obtained permission to accompany him. Thus, like Jacky Fisher, the future Admiral came under fire for the first time on land, not at sea.

What, chiefly, did he gain from his six months' experience of campaigning? Self-confidence, self-knowledge and the adaptability and judgement of men and situations that active service teaches so much more surely and quickly than any course of training. From the point of view of his career in the navy he doubted if he had done himself any good. It was only thanks to Lord Roberts' personal intervention that he had been called up to the front from a pointless job superintending two guns that had been left behind to defend Bloemfontein. Although he had won his first campaign medal with four clasps it did not escape his notice that he was the only midshipman who had fought ashore in South Africa to be omitted from the list of those recommended for early promotion. 'It has always been a mystery to me: but perhaps the personal interest Lord Roberts always took in me had something to do with it.' Not that that interest was without its compensations. In particular it led to Cunningham's first meeting with his lifelong hero and frequent companion in arms, Lieutenant, later Admiral, Walter Cowan, then serving as naval ADC to Kitchener. Of all the fire-eaters that Cunningham served with, and under, and, ultimately, over, Cowan bears the palm for length, variety and heat of service. Even then at the age of 29 he had probably, as Cunningham points out, seen more action and won more medals than most flag officers.

In the next few years Cunningham completed the sea service qualifying him for his lieutenant's examination, mostly in big ships on the Home station, and passed the necessary courses. Two points were significant for his future. Bored with having too little to do as a sub-lieutenant aboard the battleship *Implacable* he volunteered for a vacancy aboard the destroyer *Locust*: 'So began my long years in destroyers. Many a time have I blessed the notion that caused me to apply for that vacancy in the *Locust*.' She was commanded by an officer with a reputation for ruthless perfectionism such as was to surround Cunningham's own name. They got on extremely well.

The second point is complementary. Cunningham's results in his sub-lieutenant's courses, torpedoes, navigation, etc. were decent if not particularly distinguished except for the course in the subject then and long afterwards held in special veneration – gunnery. HMS *Excellent*, the gunnery school at Whale Island in Portsmouth harbour, was a byword for rigidity of discipline and disproportionate infliction of punishment. A. B. Cunningham was no soft-collared libertarian but his natural pugnacity, not to say his fierce temper, was easily roused and not so easily quieted by personal injustice or professional incompetence. He resented an atmosphere which seemed harsh and inhuman and he was not the man to disguise his feelings. The result was that he left Whale Island with a second-class certificate recording that his conduct had been unsatisfactory. This, together with a prejudice against gunnery officers and their favoured position in the service, he was to nurture as he rose to the peak of his profession.

The combination of these two strong prepossessions – for destroyers and against the gunnery establishment – found their perfect moment in the development of the navy. 'I joined Torpedo Boat 14 in the Tidal Basin at Portsmouth on 13 May 1908. Thereafter I was to serve continuously in command of torpedo craft* until 4 November 1919.' Few indeed are the periods of naval history about which such a sentence could have been written. This extraordinary career of eleven years and more in command of small ships was initiated when Jacky Fisher was First Sea Lord and might, in one sense, have been held to exemplify his raptures on the sea as an educative force qualifying a man as nothing else could for the highest command in the navy. Yet his own career, his own example, pointed in a very different direction. He had taken to specialization, first in gunnery and then in torpedoes, like a duck to water. He had urged young officers to do the same: 'If you are a gunnery man you must believe and teach that the world must be saved by gunnery and can only be saved by gunnery. If you are a torpedo man you must believe and teach the same thing about torpedoes . . . You are missionaries. Show the earnestness, if need be the fanaticism, of missionaries.' The greater part, indeed practically all, of Fisher's sea service had been as commander or flag captain aboard capital ships. But what he was always hankering for was to get his hands on the real levels of power at the Admiralty or as captain successively of Whale Island and of the torpedo establishment HMS *Vernon*.

What reserves of self-confidence, or self-reliance rather, might be built up in a strong and naturally solitary nature by the loneliness and responsibility of such experience as Cunningham's the Second War was to show in the most striking manner. But wasn't there perhaps a price to be paid? The man who wants to live alone, says

---

* Before and during the First World War this term was virtually interchangeable with destroyer.

Aristotle, is either a wild beast or a god. Andrew Cunningham was manifestly neither. And to describe a destroyer captain as living alone when for every waking minute he is watching, judging, giving orders to the officers and men under his command is almost as much of a verbal flourish as Aristotle's. Yet there is substance beneath it. A captain cannot be sociable, cannot live on terms of equality, as everyone else aboard more or less can. The strictness over minor details of dress, of every last touch of smartness in the appearance of a ship that might be entering harbour after a fair battering at sea, certainly trained commanding officers to an alertness that would be valuable in war. But did it perhaps overtrain them? Wasn't there something obsessional and narrowing in such an insistence on parade-ground minutiae? There is much evidence from Cunningham's later career that his first reaction to new ideas was hostile. He could be won over to them but his reception of them was not, like Fisher's, welcoming.

A further consequence of this hard and quasi-monastic life was the cult of the hair shirt. Anything that made life easier was *ex hypothesi* bad. Asceticism has its value in the religious and the military professions but it can drain colour and warmth from its votaries. And it can spread through the intellectual and moral system. It is difficult not to believe that it formed an important part of the doctrine now rare but common in Cunningham's day, and much later, of 'being married to the service'. This mystical union was held to render marriage in the ordinary sense tantamount to bigamy, at any rate if entered into before reaching some seniority as a commander. It received material reinforcement from the Admiralty's reluctance to pay marriage allowances beneath that rank.

Cunningham was nearly 47 when he married. The mutual society, help and comfort that the one ought to have of the other, both in prosperity and adversity, were theirs in abundance. Everyone testifies to the life-long happiness of the marriage and to the marvellously relaxed and informal hospitality of the Cunninghams, however grim the outlook and however daunting his responsibilities. 'The war stopped at his front door,' wrote Admiral

Sir Manley Power, recollecting the blackest period in the Eastern Mediterranean when he had served as Cunningham's Staff Officer (Operations). To those who knew Cunningham best the depth of his kindness and humanity, the warmth of his nature were always evident. But they were well-concealed by the manner of a martinet. The long years of continuous command were unrelieved by the throwing-off of reserve that a happy marriage makes possible. The contrast with Fisher's early career is notable. He had married, also extremely happily, at 25 and in a letter to his wife written several years later he reproaches himself for not having married her even earlier when they were both 21: 'My great mistake in life . . . we should have been quite old enough . . . and I should have been very much better in every way . . . and I should have done professionally as well.'

One thread that runs right through Cunningham's naval career is his association with the Mediterranean. Commissioning the new destroyer *Scorpion* in 1911 he was sent out there in November 1913 and spent the greater part of the war in those waters. When all eyes were turned on the North Sea and the expected sortie of the German High Seas Fleet this seemed at first a professional blank card. But the Dardanelles soon changed all that. Winston Churchill, Jacky Fisher and Andrew Cunningham were all caught in that violent eddy of history. The first two were dashed on the rocks – or so it seemed in 1915. Few would then have believed it possible that Churchill could scramble back from the shipwreck of his huge success in the most brilliant of Liberal cabinets to head the greatest of all coalitions as a Conservative. Fisher was indeed done for: but not before he had had a good run for his money. The young Andrew Cunningham, serving with the greatest distinction in that long, thankless and bloody campaign was the only one of the three who increased his stature. On 30 June 1915, still in command of *Scorpion* he was given accelerated promotion and a DSO. Both had been hard-earned. The destroyers were almost continuously at sea, pressed into every kind of service, mine-sweeping, troop-transporting, giving close support to the men in the trenches with their searchlights and their four-inch guns. Tempting targets to shore-based artillery they were often so close in as to be in range of small arms fire. In his memoirs Cunningham makes little of the dangers and the casualties but even he makes no bones about the hardships of the service and about the atrocious weather. A number of his letters from this period survive among his papers in the British Library. 'It has just stopped blowing a southerly gale which lasted six days,' he wrote on 2 January 1915, 'and now it is blowing a furious gale from the North.' Every letter expects orders for home. But on 17 March he writes: 'Our homecoming, if indeed any of us are left afloat to come home, has been postponed indefinitely.' He and those who were serving under him in the Eastern Mediterranean a quarter of a century later might have used the same words. During several months the only break in this harsh routine was a ten-day refit in Malta.

During the Gallipoli operations Cunningham must have got to know Roger Keyes, then serving as Chief-of-Staff to Admiral de Robeck. Keyes's younger brother Adrian was a close friend and colleague of Cunningham's and was commanding a destroyer in the same flotilla. Roger Keyes had already established a reputation for daring and initiative comparable to that of Cowan with whom he had served in several appointments before the war. These two men set the standards to which Cunningham aspired. To the end of the Gallipoli campaign Keyes urged the taking of the Straits by a purely naval assault, a course against which his Admiral, de Robeck, consistently advised. Cunningham refrains from any criticism of the planning and conduct of Gallipoli but it seems probable that he would have respected de Robeck's judgement while admiring Keyes's fire.

At any rate on his return to England in 1918 after the months of uneventful Mediterranean convoy duty that followed the final evacuation of Gallipoli it was to Keyes's flag, then flying over the Dover Patrol, that to his great delight he was appointed. Keyes offered him the chance of taking the old battleship *Swiftsure* to block Ostend as a follow-up to his own operations against Zeebrugge. Cunningham picked his crew and threw himself into the preparation for an enterprise that, to his bitter disappointment, had at the last minute to be abandoned. But that Keyes should have chosen him showed what his reputation was. Had the war not ended only a few weeks later it seems highly probable that under such a commander Cunningham would have had other opportunities worthy of his skill and daring.

Only a few months later, he found himself quite unexpectedly under the command of his other hero, Cowan, who had been ordered to the Baltic. Early in 1919 the situation there was dangerous and confused: the Bolshevik armies and a much more formidable German force that disclaimed allegiance to the government that had signed the armistice were disputing with each other and with the newly emergent nationalist movements of Latvia, Lithuania, Estonia and Finland the control of what had been the westernmost territories of the Tsarist Empire. The unpredictable course of affairs, the uncertainty of British policy and the vagueness of the instructions from Whitehall left Cowan plenty of scope for vigorous and exciting action. Captain Geoffrey Bennett's book *Cowan's War* gives a clear account of events into which it is not necessary to go. Cowan's enthusiasm for Cunningham's services was expressed in his report and in the award, within a year, of a second bar to his DSO.

One incident that Cunningham records, small in itself, is perhaps revealing. Returning to harbour one day he was overtaken by thick fog. The waters were unfamiliar, the swept channel narrow. He asked for and obtained permission to anchor until the weather cleared. Reporting aboard the flagship he found Cowan displeased. Destroyers were not, in his view, to be handled so cautiously. Cunningham, then only a fairly junior Commander, stood his ground against the Vice-Admiral. 'We parted in some disagreement.' Like so many of his phrases this understates the moral courage here shown. Both Keyes and Cowan had been from earliest youth passionate fox-hunters in an era when riding straight across country, no matter what the obstacles, was held to be the true ethos of the sport. It was this type of courage, this exultant blindness to danger, that both exemplified. Cunningham never hunted, was indeed no horseman and not much of a games-player. Fishing and golf, those reflective, individualist pursuits, were his preferred amusements.

With this appointment the eleven years in command of destroyers came to an end. It can hardly be disputed, certainly Cunningham would not have disputed it, that this was the most formative experience of his career. To it he would unhesitatingly ascribe the credit for his subsequent success. He never specialized in torpedoes or navigation or signals: at that time few destroyer-men did. Gunnery was, as we have seen, anathema. He did not acquire languages or serve with foreign navies. He was, in the idiom of the wardroom, a salthorse, a seaman pure and simple. A friendly critic who had served under him successfully, Admiral J. H. Godfrey, told his biographer, Oliver Warner, that this was a great pity as specialization would have broadened his mind:

> Years and years of destroyer work . . . association with other destroyer captains of Lieutenant-Commander's rank, all little tin gods, produces autocrats at all levels. It is a tribute to the greatness of A.B.C. that he didn't succumb completely . . . By neglecting the sublime (to quote Kempenfelt) aspects of his profession he threw his career out of balance but tried to protect himself by belittling everything but destroyer work and command.

In some moods Cunningham might have agreed with him. Vice-Admiral Sir Francis Pridham records his remark on the eve of the Second War when he knew that he was likely to become Commander-in-Chief in the Mediterranean. 'I think the Admiralty has treated me badly keeping me twenty-four years in destroyers.' He was here adding his periods of service as Captain of a Destroyer Flotilla, at the Scottish Destroyer Base at Port Edgar, and as Rear Admiral Commanding Destroyers in the Mediterranean Fleet during the twenties and thirties.

That service has been chronicled by Cunningham himself and by his biographers. It will be, no doubt, further surveyed in the volume of Cunningham papers which the Navy Records Society intends to publish in the near future. Here a selective view will best serve the purpose of this essay.

The year 1926 saw the first great alteration of course in his career. Cowan who had been appointed Commander-in-Chief on the American and West Indies Station invited Cunningham to join him as his Flag Captain and Chief Staff Officer. The flagship, the *Calcutta*, was a cruiser, a class of vessel in which Cunningham had not served since his very early days. And the duties of a Chief Staff Officer might seem daunting to an officer who had not attended the Staff Course, let alone served in a junior staff appointment. In fact it proved an ideal apprenticeship to Flag Rank. The main function of the squadron was to show the flag in South America as well as in the West Indies and above all to cultivate good relations with Canada and the United States. This meant a strenuous life of seatime followed, as the anchor went down, by non-stop social activity. In all this Cunningham acquitted himself admirably.

To unexpected difficulties he rose with his usual professionalism. He earned Cowan's approbation for bringing the *Calcutta* into the basin at Montreal with a six-knot current swirling past the entrance. Her sister ship, commanded by an officer who had specialized in navigation, bruised her bows severely against the harbour wall as she followed her in. Cowan and Cunningham shook their heads over the effects of specialization. Cunningham showed his outstanding quality as a seaman in his handling of the ship when she was caught by a hurricane in harbour at Ireland Island, Bermuda. His own account in *A Sailor's Odyssey*, exciting, amusing and well-written, is mildly self-critical. Cowan's, in a private letter written to Keyes four days later, shows what his superior thought:

They hadn't had an Oct hurricane here for 150 years and it travelled at 300 miles a day faster than is normal for these storms.

The anemometer with the brake hard on registered 138 mph and then broke.

My *Calcutta* was lashed with 28 hawsers to the dockyard & 6 of them were 12″ hurricane hawsers. In under 2 minutes in that same gust 27 of them went & she had as well an anchor down & steam of course on the main engines. She blew away bows first & drove on to the outer pier end & stove in 2 plates. *Very* splendidly handled by Cunningham and as fine and high-spirited a crew as I've ever sailed with – they hung on to her there – 2 officers with lifebuoys & lines nipped in & swam the few yards down wind to her & so they got other lines to her. It was just the right sort of officer-like example and prompt action that you & I have learnt to watch for I think . . .

Cowan's letter is written for the eyes and imagination of a fellow seaman. Cunningham's account makes everything clear to the inexperienced, notably the fact that the Bermudas are ringed with reefs and it was against one of these that the *Calcutta* was about to be dashed broadside on when he brought her head up against the stone pier at the harbour entrance. But it is the last sentence I have quoted from Cowan's letter that contains the root of the matter, the first article of naval belief to which Nelson, Jacky Fisher and Cunningham himself would all have said 'Amen'.

It is in this context applied not directly to Cunningham himself but to two of his (unnamed) officers. But in any service worth the name the conduct of subordinates reflects the quality of their commander. Cunningham certainly thought so, and often, and vigorously, voiced the Napoleonic axiom that there were no bad troops, only bad officers. In the present instance he uses the incident to celebrate in a simple paragraph the life and service of his second-in-command and by implication gives him the credit. Generosity of spirit was hardly masked by the red face with its piercing blue-eyed stare and the martinet manner.

Two years of cheerful, if for Cunningham's taste too convivial, service were enough. The incessant entertainment demanded by flag-showing would have taxed a more robust digestion than his. It was only the amount of seatime that kept him healthy and relieved the strain on his serious and retiring nature. That and, of course, the close association which grew into close friendship with Sir Walter Cowan.

What followed was a no less valuable but very different preparation for the exigencies of high command. 'I look on my year at the Imperial Defence College as one of the most interesting and valuable I have ever spent.' This is a remarkable judgement from one who prided himself on not having attended a Staff Course, not having specialized, not having sat behind a desk in Whitehall. For the IDC was all these things raised to a higher power. Its object was to promote the intercourse of the most promising officers of middle rank in the three services both with each other and with their counterparts in the civil and diplomatic services. The range of subject matter extended to economics and foreign affairs as well as the likely developments in every branch of warfare. The atmosphere was intellectual and argumentative. If there was a practical side it consisted in visiting all kinds of institutions and establishments where anything with a plausible claim to development or pioneering might be going on or, in Cunningham's case, being taken up in an aeroplane for the first time in his life in order to resolve an argument about the searchlight defences of London. His adversary and pilot on that occasion was the future Lord Portal, subsequently Chief of Air Staff from 1940 to the end of the war.

It is difficult not to agree with Admiral Godfrey's judgement that the Admiralty ought to have seen to it that he was exposed to such experience much earlier in his career. As it was his natural intelligence and integrity of mind had to struggle against a carapace of small-mindedness, distrust of innovation, belief in the moral value of physical discomfort and, not least, horror of expenditure. 'Too Rolls-Royce and velvet-arsed' – his characteristic dismissal of any scheme that might make life easier or cost money reflects the years in destroyers as well as the long line of his Scottish ancestry.

From the IDC he moved to yet another new field, the command of the *Rodney*, one of the largest, most powerful and most modern battleships afloat. Cunningham records with approval the admonition of the Admiral commanding the 1st Battle Squadron after he had shown him round: 'On no account allow yourself to become entangled in the technicalities of this great ship.' This represents the opposite pole of doctrine from that exemplified by Mountbatten who a few years later was to pride himself on his ability as Director of the Signals Department to perform every function carried out by those under his command right down to the O/D Sparker who had to read Morse at 23 words a minute. Admiral Drax's injunction has a grand simplicity: but might it not conceal the natural reluctance of a weather-beaten veteran to come to grips with the rapidly increasing complications of modern sea warfare? This trait could certainly be observed in Cunningham. Admiral Godfrey criticizes the obstinacy with which he maintained that there was nothing in the art of commanding a big ship that could not be learnt from commanding a small one. As in his opinions on staff courses and specialization a self-defensive growl may be suspected.

The *Rodney* was a plum command and her officers numbered several rising stars. Her commander, Robert Burnett, was to achieve an outstanding record of success in action fighting convoys through to North Russia. But it was the Gunnery Officer, Geoffrey Oliver, with whom Cunningham found and retained the closest affinity, in spite of his violent prejudice against the gunnery school, of which Oliver was perhaps the most brilliant product. Oliver, like Cunningham, was the son of a science professor, was not, like Cowan or Keyes, a fox-hunter or a polo player but a technical specialist of first-rate quality who also possessed gifts of leadership, humour and charm of character. His sketch of service under Cunningham achieves a convincing likeness:

I suppose A.B.C.'s most conspicuous quality was his intense spirit of attack – or the offensive, if you prefer it – which he brought to bear on whatever he undertook. He could be, and often was, the most biting driver; but never without acute perception that the thing could be done the way he wanted it, and, what is more, would be done . . . Behind all his ferocity was the kindest heart imaginable. I think it was these two 'opposites', laced with an almost boyish sense of humour, that captivated and bound us to him.

At almost the same moment as he took command of the *Rodney*, Cunningham embarked on an even more successful venture – that of matrimony. Lady Cunningham was to accompany her husband on all his future appointments and the happiness and hospitality that a stream of guests from cabinet ministers to midshipmen recall must have done much to bear him up in the trials that lay ahead. The care he took of her may be judged by his refusing Churchill's offer of a passage in the *Duke of York* on his appointment to the Joint Services Commission in Washington in the summer of 1942. 'His invitation did not include my wife, and I did not think she would care to fly the Atlantic without me.'*

Cunningham left the *Rodney* in December 1930 having commanded her for exactly a year. He had won golden opinions in a post that clearly marked him out for rapid promotion. He went on to serve as Commodore of Chatham Barracks, a responsible but unexciting appointment and in the autumn of 1932 he duly got his flag. From 1934 he served for two years as Rear-Admiral Destroyers in the Mediterranean. Everyone admired the brilliance with which he handled large numbers of ships manoeuvring at high speed but that after all was what everyone expected. No new professional ground was being broken. At the same age and the same seniority Jacky Fisher had become a national figure, known to the Sovereign and regarded by politicians and others in the front rank of public life as a force to be reckoned with. He had transformed the weapons of the Royal Navy and was already clearing the way to revolutionize ship design. He had been Captain of the gunnery school, had served in the Admiralty and was about to join the Board as Controller. In

---

*In fact Churchill's journey to Washington in June 1942 was made by air in a Boeing Clipper, not by battleship.

the middle 1930s no one outside the navy had heard of Cunningham.

But there was no doubt that in the service he had, in spite of his horror of anything approaching self-advertisement, established a notable reputation. His long service in destroyers may have unbalanced his career as Admiral Godfrey suggested and as Cunningham himself seems sometimes to have thought. But it was, as his Chief of Staff Admiral Dick emphasized to me, the foundation of that career. His performance as a Destroyer Captain became a legend in the service, as ship-handler, disciplinarian, tactical innovator and above all as a leader. Continuous experience of command such as his is an impossibility in the Royal Navy of the late twentieth century just as it was in the navy of Charles II. Even Nelson in what, seen from a distance, looks an almost unbroken series of naval wars, knew long frustrating years when there were no ships to be had. Both Fisher and Cunningham were fortunate in their historical contexts.

When Cunningham hauled down his flag as Rear-Admiral Destroyers in 1936 he had his first taste of what sea officers of earlier generations had had to swallow. There would be no appointment available, he was told, for an officer of his rank for at least two years. Coming as he had from the Mediterranean where the prospect of war with Italy over Abyssinia had at one point seemed imminent this sudden sentence to idleness and futility was the more galling. His Commander-in-Chief, Admiral Sir William Fisher, had been confident that he could defeat Mussolini's navy. The fleet base had been moved from Malta to Alexandria since the Sicilian airfields were a mere 60 miles from the Grand Harbour. Cunningham had drawn up plans for intercepting Italian troop-convoys and had specially asked for Philip Vian, newly promoted Captain, to be sent out to take command of one of his destroyer divisions. In all this Cunningham and Fisher (brother of H.A.L. the historian and no relation of Jacky's) had worked in the closest harmony, a harmony cemented by their disgust at the timidity shown by the Chiefs of Staff in London who doubted the Mediterranean Fleet's sufficiency to take on the Italians. They had no doubts on the subject and planned to launch an immediate offensive.

From 1936 to 1940 and 1941 looks a short step in the hindsight of history. It can hardly have looked like that to an ardent fighting leader condemned to mowing the lawns at Bishops Waltham, the house in Hampshire that he took on his return. Would things have turned out differently, one wonders – and perhaps Cunningham wondered – if instead of going out to the Mediterranean as Rear Admiral Destroyers he had gone as William Fisher's Chief of Staff? This had been very much on the cards. Towards the end of his time as Commodore of Chatham Barracks, Cunningham had been invited to dine with the Commander-in-Chief the Nore to meet Sir William. The two men had been put next to each other and had had a long and, from Cunningham's recollection, argumentative discussion of various professional matters. They did not get on. Fisher's service nickname, the Great Agrippa, half-laughingly suggests both his undoubted impressiveness and his own awareness of it. It was not till several days later that Cunningham's host told him that Fisher had asked for this opportunity of sizing him up as a candidate. Rear-Admiral Destroyers was certainly a more congenial appointment, but to have been Chief of Staff might have been a useful qualification for further employment.

As it turned out Cunningham was not out to grass for more than a few months. Early in 1937 he was appointed Chairman of an Admiralty committee charged with studying the ventilation of ships. This sounds a task more appropriate to Sir Edwin Chadwick in the age of Queen Victoria. In fact it was an ideal introduction to the corridors of naval bureaucracy and provided a brief wide enough to encompass such subjects as cafeteria-messing in big ships, safety measures against gases released by explosions and other details of construction as well as the obvious, perennial question of how to keep ever-increasing numbers of men healthy in necessarily cramped, confined conditions. Every technical advance, radar, asdic, improved electronic systems of control, meant more and more specialist officers and ratings coming aboard vessels where space was already at a premium. The work therefore involved a great deal of visiting of ships, shore-establishments and firms who were producing the latest equipment. It brought Cunningham into regular contact – the committee met at the Admiralty two or three times a week – with scientists and civil servants of some eminence. It prepared him, perhaps better than a tour of duty as a Chief of Staff would have done, for the responsibilities for decision in unfamiliar matters that would soon be thrust upon him.

About the end of June on one of his days at the Admiralty, Cunningham heard that Sir Geoffrey Blake, second-in-command of the Mediterranean Fleet and commander of the battle-cruiser squadron, had been taken to hospital in Malta. A week later he was offered the post on a temporary basis till Blake was well again. Cunningham at once accepted and was in Malta by mid-July.

Blake, an officer of rare quality and by general recollection a most winning personality, did not make a full recovery and was lost to the active list. Cunningham was confirmed in the appointment and thus found himself yet again playing one of the leading parts in a full dress-rehearsal on the stage he was so soon to make his own. No flag officer in the history of the Royal Navy has known the Mediterranean over so long a period, in so many moods, under so many constellations of fortune. It was not only the sea, the ports, the coasts, the islands, the anchorages, the winds and the weather. It was also the men whom he was so soon to fight against or fight alongside or whose neutrality he was to keep as benevolent as he could. The Italians, the French and the Turks were the main powers with whom he was concerned. But the Greeks and the Yugoslavs had to be considered. The Spaniards obviously were more the preoccupation of the Commander-in-Chief at Gibraltar. But their civil war, then raging, involved the Mediterranean Fleet in the protection of British shipping, especially against Italian submarines which were supporting General Franco by acts of undeclared war.

Cunningham was no linguist. It seems at first sight surprising that so intelligent and active-minded a man could have spent so much of his life in the Mediterranean without acquiring the most elementary knowledge of French or Italian. But his great powers of observation, his shrewdness of judgement, and his gift for getting on with people served him well. It was in 1937 that he first met the French admiral commanding in North Africa, Esteva, with whom he was to form a friendship that survived the intolerable strains imposed by the surrender of 1940. Doubtless Cunningham particularly approved the more than monastic asceticism of his *train de vie*: 'A tough man and highly religious, he rose each morning at 5.15 and went to mass, followed at seven o'clock by a meagre breakfast of coffee, dry toast and an orange, with nothing more till lunch.' Nothing Rolls-Royce or velvet-arsed about that.

If Esteva was of a temperament and tastes naturally congenial to Cunningham, the Italian admiral Riccardi, whom he was to defeat at the battle of Matapan four years later, was the reverse:

We lunched on board the *Conte di Cavour* with Admiral Riccardi, and came to the conclusion that he must have embarked the whole catering staff and band from one of the best hotels in Rome, so distinguished was his entertainment. Afterwards he took us round his palatial and highly decorated private apartments . . . On the whole we liked Admiral Riccardi and the senior officers, who were most courteous and pleasant. The younger officers, however, were ill-mannered and boorish.

It will be seen that A.B.C. allowed his prejudices to colour but not to shape his judgements.

Perhaps the most important of all the personal contacts established by Cunningham's unexpected relief of Geoffrey Blake was that with his Commander-in-Chief, Sir Dudley Pound. The two men were to be so totally dependent on each other in the early disastrous years of the war, when Pound was First Sea Lord and Cunningham Commander-in-Chief at Alexandria, that this first close collaboration was timely indeed. Cunningham's tribute to Pound in *A Sailor's Odyssey* is generous and evidently sincere. 'In lapidary inscriptions a man is not upon oath.' But the careful qualifications show that Cunningham was paying the man he was to succeed both as Commander-in-Chief Mediterranean and as First Sea Lord the compliment of discriminating assessment. The nub of the matter is that Cunningham did not put him in the top class as a sea officer, as a commander of a fleet or as one of that invaluable band who trained the navy for the coming war but he did give him full marks as an administrator and has no hesitation in saying that as First Sea Lord in 1939 he was the right man in the right place. Clearly the two men got on well. Cunningham goes out of his way to emphasize that Pound always treated him as a friend and as a colleague who enjoyed his complete trust. He lets it be perceived that not all his fellow commanders were so fortunate.

Their first private exchange set the tone for all that was to follow. Pound made it clear that he considered that a second-in-command had a duty to tell his chief what he thought, particularly if he disagreed with a decision or felt anxiety about any shortcoming in the fleet. This was exactly Cunningham's view of the matter and in no time at all he was coaching the Commander-in-Chief in the correct pronunciation of the Serbo–Croat greeting 'God bless you, my children', which the inspecting officer had to shout before passing down the ranks of a guard of honour. Visits to the countries of the central and eastern Mediterranean, tours of duty off Valencia and Barcelona took up much of the time. But the true themes of this overture were the personal contacts established with the future First Sea Lord and with our French allies.

The appointment ended in the summer of 1938 during which Cunningham was told that the new First Sea Lord, Sir Roger Backhouse, had asked for him at the Admiralty as Deputy Chief of Naval Staff. He took up this post in October, just after the Munich Crisis, and found that everyone from the First Sea Lord down shared his own conviction that war was imminent. Backhouse worked far too hard and what was worse refused to delegate. Cunningham, who had neither training nor aptitude for staff work, could hardly have had a less auspicious introduction to it. It was only with difficulty that he persuaded his chief to let him handle all the issues arising from the Spanish Civil War which was fresh in his experience. And in a few months Backhouse had incapacitated himself by overwork. Thus Cunningham found himself doing duty for the First Sea Lord as well as his own work. To crown everything the outstandingly able Third Sea Lord suddenly collapsed and shortly died. It soon became plain too that Backhouse would not recover.

Serious illness and sudden death had within a year disrupted the succession to the principal posts in the navy. Sir William Fisher, natural choice for First Sea Lord, had died suddenly as Commander-in-Chief Portsmouth in June 1937. A month later, as we have seen, Geoffrey Blake's illness created an opening for Cunningham. Now with the Board of Admiralty deprived of its two most important members on the eve of a major war a reconstitution of the hierarchy was imperative. Pound was summoned to succeed Backhouse and Cunningham was invited to take his place in the Mediterranean with immediate promotion to the rank of Admiral. He thus found himself back in Malta a year after he had left it but this time as Commander-in-Chief.

The three months before the declaration of war were put to good use. The closest contacts were established with the French, not only with the navy but also with General Weygand of whom Cunningham held the highest opinion. The Commander in charge of plans, Royer Dick, who had been partly brought up in France, formed a close friendship with the future Admiral Auboyneau whose superior, Admiral Godfroy, was married to an English wife. All this helped to turn the scale a year later in the dangers and difficulties created by the fall of France. Italy, it was agreed, was certain to come in on the side of Germany when the time was right. What was far from certain was how far Turkey might be induced to weight her neutrality in favour of the Axis or of the Western powers. Cunningham was therefore ordered to take the fleet to Istanbul on a ceremonial visit which was to include a personal interview with President Inönu and Field Marshal Chakmak in Ankara. The warmth and humanity of the Admiral's personality evidently endeared him to his hosts whom he took to at once. 'Such a charming little man, speaking broken English which he has learnt in the last year. He was embarrassingly friendly, seizing my hand in both of his while he expressed haltingly how pleased he was to see us. I was much taken with him and it was difficult to realise that he, in his younger days, had been a very truculent soldier who nearly fell foul of us at Chanak after the war. I suppose he was in the right of it – we were in his country, occupying it.'

This sketch of the President, taken from a private letter written at the time, shows something of the attractiveness and straightfor-wardness of Cunningham's nature and perhaps a touch of that detachment and magnanimity that was to characterize his conduct under difficulties and dilemmas as agonising as any faced by a British commander in the Second World War. What the letter also shows is a far more rarely glimpsed responsiveness. He and Lady Cunningham were taken up into the dome of Santa Sophia where the American Professor Whitamore was at work uncovering the mosaics. Cunningham was clearly fascinated by what Whitamore showed him: 'He had such great thoughts and ideas which he kept shooting at us.'

Less than a month later war was declared. Cunningham was standing on the foremost fifteen-inch gun turret of the battleship *Malaya* watching the finish of a race in the squadron regatta when he was handed the signal. 'I never expected when war was declared to have nothing to do but go ashore and have tea with my wife,' he wrote that day to his aunt. 'I fear it had to come with such a set of ruffians governing Germany. Italy not coming in has rather left us high and dry out here . . . Perhaps it was the excellence of our preparations which has made them keep out.'

Naturally the greater part of his forces were immediately required for service in the many theatres where German activity threatened our sea-routes. Cunningham's function was to watch and wait. Off went the battle squadron, his aircraft-carrier and most of his destroyers. The sense of being on the sidelines, of being a passenger even, stirred a morbid, puritanical streak conspicuously absent when danger and action were in the air. 'This island [Malta] badly wants a bomb dropped on it', he wrote on 21 January. 'The Governor has been pushed by the Maltese into doing away with most of the wartime restrictions so cars roar about all night and places of entertainment remain open as they like.' He thought it wrong that young officers and their wives should go dancing in night-clubs at so serious a moment. A visit a week later from the abstemious Admiral Esteva – who had now refined his austerities yet further: '*Dejeuner*, coffee, dry toast and an orange at 7 a.m., then he works the whole day till 11 p.m.' – redressed the balance. Yet even at this mortifying period of enforced inactivity reason and magnanimity kept breaking in. Six weeks after the beginning of the war he and Lady Cunningham gave a dinner-party for the young wives of officers whose ships had been recalled from the Mediterranean. His neighbour at table evidently had a refreshing disregard for rank and protocol:

> One young woman very much against all war for whatever cause. I told her her generation were being called on to make sacrifices so that their children might lead peaceful lives but she would have none of it. Couldn't see that wars ever led to anything becoming better.
>
> I must say she had some right on her side as I don't think the Great War led to anything better and now it's to do all over again. I feel we mishandled the peace . . .

How many commanding officers, let alone Commanders-in-Chief, would have listened to so courteously and represented so fairly such arguments?

As regards the political and military conduct of the war there were moral and personal norms – loyalty, innocence, a scholarly refusal to pass judgement without being certain of all the relevant facts – that underlay all his estimates of people and of their actions. This approach was tempered, sharpened, by canniness and by a questioning shrewdness. 'It rather serves us right', he wrote to his aunt a week after the outbreak of war, 'ever trying to make an agreement with those wretched Russians. However they and the Germans will be fighting among themselves before they finish.' Yet he did not share the enthusiasm of Chamberlain and Halifax for declaring war on Russia in support of the Finns. 'Easy enough to say but it might queer our pitch with the Turks who do not wish to fight Russia' (7 January 1940). Fortunately for his peace of mind he cannot have been fully informed of the vacillation, ineptitude and dishonour that characterized British and French policy over the Norwegian episode. If he had been he would surely have been better pleased by Churchill's elevation to the Premiership which was its immediate and direct outcome. 'What do you think of all this racket in Parliament? To me it seems they think more of politics than they do of the war. Winston has got what he has been intriguing for. I don't know if he will stick the course: he lives at a high rate' (11 May 1940).

Now that we are nearing the end of the twentieth century Churchill's place in the national pantheon seems firmly established, somewhere along with King Alfred, Oliver Cromwell and the two Pitts. To my own generation which served in the war he seemed an unquestionable, unshakable, part of the scheme of things. Like the weather or the movement of the stars. To the extent that we were politically conscious or critical we should probably have assented to Lady Churchill's letter to Asquith a quarter of a century earlier piercing to the heart of the matter: 'Winston may have his faults but he has the deadliness to fight Germany.'

To my parents' generation – to which Cunningham belonged – a very different perspective presented itself. In Edwardian politics and society he had given grounds for the opinion that he was an adventurer and a bounder. Of his dazzling abilities – his 'hundred horse-power mind' as Baldwin called it – there could be no two opinions. But what would a naval officer of Cunningham's years and experience think of his judgement in bringing Jacky Fisher back to the Admiralty and then failing to make sure of his support for or to take account of his reasons for opposing the assault on the Dardanelles? Cunningham had seen, had felt, the price exacted in men and ships for this expensive failure. He must have heard of Churchill's proposal, received by his colleagues in Asquith's cabinet with roars of incredulous laughter, that he should take personal command of the Antwerp sector where the Royal Naval Division had been landed in the autumn of 1914. The omens, viewed from a flagship of the Royal Navy, were by no means all favourable, even if he did not know, as he probably did not, of Churchill's responsibility as Chancellor of the Exchequer for the 'No major war within ten years' rule which had inhibited expenditure on defence until 1934. The tub-thumping over India and the championing of Edward VIII's right to marry Mrs Simpson had certainly not enhanced the reputation of Churchill's political judgement. Probably unfairly both could be seen as the desperate throws of an adventurer who feels age creeping on and the last prospects of power steadily receding.

All this is offered in an attempt to understand the development of the relations between the two men who rendered such incomparable service to their country but did not always render justice to each other. Undoubtedly the last part of the passage just quoted, unselfconscious, unconsidered, casually thrown off, yields one valuable clue: 'He lives at a high rate.' There is a great gulf fixed between those who regard personal expenditure as probably sinful and certainly vulgar, and those who regard carefulness in such matters as mean and underbred. Snobbery, overt and inverted, comes into it as does the antithesis, so deep in our national character, between Puritan and Cavalier. Churchill was a Cavalier to end all Cavaliers, forever hob-nobbing with dukes and plutocrats in a sybaritic atmosphere of cigars and champagne.

The relationship between them began unhappily. All through the winter of 1939 and the early spring of 1940 Cunningham's energies had been devoted to joint planning with the French and the Turks against a German descent through the Balkans which the authorities in London regarded as a likely accompaniment to Italy's entry into the war. By the time that Churchill succeeded to the Premiership, Italy's declaration of war was expected from day to day. Cunningham's principal responsibilities were first to make sure that none of the heavy Italian traffic passing through Suez should sink itself and block the canal or take the opportunity of sabotaging the harbours at Port Said or Alexandria, now the base of a hastily reinforced Mediterranean Fleet. Second to this came the elaborate preparations for blockading and ultimately seizing the Dodecanese, then in Italian possession, and protecting the great harbours of Asia minor, notably Smyrna. Crete was to be occupied at once if Greece was attacked but not otherwise. And all this was to be done with a total absence of air-cover. In the dire situation of May 1940 fighters could not even be spared for the defence of Malta which, as expected, came under immediate and sustained attack from the Sicilian airfields as soon as Italy declared war on 10 June.

To thread his way through this cat's cradle of commitments and contingencies in the Eastern Mediterranean Cunningham signalled his disposition of forces. Until these had been met and until he received air-cover for operations against the sea-route from Italy to Libya he did not propose to attack that traffic with his main force. Churchill read the signal and let it be known that he thought the Commander-in-Chief was insufficiently imbued with the offensive spirit. Dudley Pound at once tried to take the sting out of the Prime Minister's message. But there are some words that cannot be unsaid. Eleven years later reflecting on the exchange Cunningham wrote:

> It was in the sort of 'prodding' message received by me on 5 June that Mr Churchill was often so ungracious and hasty. We realized, of course, the terrible mental and physical strain under which he was labouring; but so were we. Such messages to those who were doing their utmost with straitened resources were not an encouragement, merely an annoyance. Moreover, as they implied that something was lacking in the direction and leadership, they did positive harm. If such messages were really

necessary, if Commanders-in-Chief on the spot who knew all the risks and the chances were not prepared to get at the enemy on every possible occasion, the recipients ought not to have been in the position they held.

This classic statement of the principles of control in war was to be made good in Cunningham's practice, both towards his own subordinate commanders and, harder still, towards further attempts at back-seat driving from the Admiralty or 10 Downing Street.

It is a remarkable, and largely unnoticed, warrant of Cunningham's excellent relations with his French allies that even in the early months of 1940 when the British Mediterranean Fleet was down to three light cruisers and a handful of destroyers while the French fleet still boasted four battleships, six eight-inch or six-inch cruisers and a handsome destroyer force there was never any question of the French admiral replacing the British in the joint command. In the tragic events that now followed that trust shone bright.

'The German invasion of Holland and Belgium just leaves one speechless . . . the cold-blooded wickedness of it to me is frightful,' he wrote on 11 May. 'Weygand told me yesterday that it was what the French generals have been praying for and that all preparations have been made to meet it. I hope that's true.' A fortnight later he greeted Weygand's appointment to command the armies of France with enthusiasm. 'I have had a lot to do with him out here and have the greatest admiration for him.' Even after everything was over he still stood by his opinion:

You ask me what I think of Weygand. I was absolutely flabbergasted when I heard he was one of the leading men concerned in the surrender of France. I still have the highest opinion of him, such a fine little man . . . It's queer how they caved in. The French admiral here said at the time that it was a case of two very old men driving to Bordeaux through crowds of refugees that must have decided them to give in.

Of course we had our troubles here with the French ships but thank goodness we were able to settle the matter without bloodshed. I never approved of the Oran business and got rather unpopular saying so.

That letter was written to his aunt on 9 September. The last paragraph quoted ranks among the great understatements of English history. It conceals a sustained moral heroism that deserves to be better known and better celebrated.

The Italian declaration of war became known in Alexandria at 7 p.m. on 10 June. Within hours the main British force put to sea for an offensive sweep to the westward while Godfroy took his French cruisers north to the Aegean and the Dodecanese. No Italian surface ships were encountered though there was some submarine activity and mines were laid by the enemy off the approaches to Alexandria. Three days later the ships were back in harbour, only to sail again six days later to bombard Bardia. A French battleship and two French cruisers took part in this operation. Two days later, on 22 June, the French government signed the armistice. On that day Cunningham had planned to sail in force to the waters between Italy and Libya and to bombard Southern Sicily. For less than a fortnight of active warfare he hadn't let much grass grow under his feet.

The sadness he felt at the deprivation of French support was soon overtaken by consternation, even horror, at the measure proposed by the Admiralty for dealing with the situation. The main units of the French navy had been sent abroad to North and West African ports. By far the most important concentration of strength was at Oran in the Western Mediterranean. To prevent it falling into German or Italian hands a considerable fleet, named Force H, was hastily assembled at Gibraltar under the command of Cunningham's old friend and term-mate, Sir James Somerville. Next to Oran the most formidable French force was that which lay alongside Cunningham's own fleet in Alexandria. Command of the Mediterranean certainly, that of the Atlantic possibly, could not be wrested from our enemies unless the benevolence or at least the neutrality of these two fleets was assured.

So good were the relations, so deep the personal friendships, so absolute the trust between the French and the British admirals in the fleets and bases that guarded the Mediterranean that Cunningham and his colleagues had no doubt that a satisfactory agreement could be reached. There was not a trace of pro-German or pro-Italian feeling in the French fleet: rather there was a bitterness and a ferocity against the barbarians who were overrunning their country. Cunningham's feelings when, on 29 June, he was informed of a plan for seizing the French ships at Oran and Alexandria by force, do not have to be imagined since he has stated them himself.

> To me the idea was utterly repugnant. The officers and men in the French squadron were our friends. We had had many most cordial social contacts with them, and they had fought alongside us. Vice-Admiral Godfroy, moreover, was a man of honour in whom we could place implicit faith. Suddenly and without warning to attack and board his ships, and in the course of it probably to inflict many casualties on his sailors, appeared to me to be an act of sheer treachery which was as injudicious as it was unnecessary.

Words like honour and treachery are now apt to embarrass people a little, as if a total stranger were to beard them in the street and ask if they were saved. Falstaff's great soliloquy on the subject of honour anticipated with incomparable wit the view of the matter to which the heirs of the linguistic philosophers have accommodated themselves. Perhaps Cunningham's opinion, recorded a few pages back, of the Nazi invasion of Holland and Belgium struck the reader as naïve. But honour was as real to him as the cannon's mouth was to Falstaff, as real as it was to Falstaff's contemporaries Hotspur and Henry V. Without such an animating principle courage in the face of superior force amounts to no more than brutish defiance.

Of this sort of courage Cunningham was to show the most

dogged instances in the history of the Royal Navy since Monck led out his fleet on four successive days to face the superior Dutch forces off the mouth of the Thames in 1666. But what he showed now was courage of a rarer kind. He did not disguise from his superiors what he felt to be the disgrace of such action against his companions in arms. And he argued most powerfully that even in a pragmatic view it would be militarily both crazy in itself and counterproductive in its consequences. 'If ships are to be seized, what is the object? If it is to prevent ships falling into enemy hands, that has already been achieved.'

The second clause of Cunningham's signal to the Admiralty on 30 June showed with unanswerable rationality that this Emperor of a policy had no clothes. He went on: 'I am convinced that the French would resist most strongly, so that if it is desired to obtain ships for our own use it is unlikely to be achieved by forcible seizure. Such action would be more likely to result in ships being scuttled at their moorings, a harbour filled with wrecks, and unnecessary British and French casualties.'

He then underlined the political, and military, consequences of such proceedings in neighbouring French possessions in the Middle East such as Syria and French Somaliland and the Canal itself, pointing out that as the flow of pay, supplies and food dried up the ships were most likely to 'drop into our hands'.

In conclusion he moved from his own command to a wider criticism of the plan: 'This appreciation makes no allowance for the repercussions which would follow the use of force at Oran. I am strongly opposed to such action there if it can possibly be avoided. I am not in full possession of the facts, but may remark that the whole of the friendly French element may be alienated, and in particular I would mention the effect in North Africa where friendly attitudes may greatly affect naval operations later on.'

The firm, temperate, rational tone of this signal had its effect. On 1 July the Admiralty replied, authorizing the offer of various terms for obtaining possession of or neutralizing the ships. If none of these were acceptable the French should be given the final option of taking their ships out to sea and scuttling them in deep water. No threat of violence was mentioned. But it was still a prominent and terrible feature of the instructions given to Admiral Somerville for dealing with the ships at Oran, of which Cunningham was kept fully informed. Somerville was to appear off Oran on 3 July and demand acceptance. Cunningham was instructed to present his alternatives to Godfroy in Alexandria at the early hour of 7 a.m. on that day so that there might be a chance of securing his agreement before he heard of the hideous events that looked only too probable at the other end of the Mediterranean.

On 2 July, 'a day of tense anxiety', Cunningham acquainted all his flag officers and captains with what was happening and made preparations for attempting the seizure of the ships if, against his strong objection, the Government ordered it. The French admiral received the invitation to come aboard the flagship at an hour whose unseasonableness must have warned him to expect no easy colloquy.

The hour may have been uncivilized but his reception wasn't. The Royal Marine guard and band were at attention on the quarterdeck. The bos'n piped the admiral over the side; arms were presented and the Marseillaise floated out on the awakening harbour. Down in the after cabin of the *Warspite* the two parties sat in armchairs, not ranged on opposite sides of a table. Cunningham took Godfroy through the proposals, noting his reactions with a delicacy not usually associated with his spirit of aggressive leadership. To the first, Godfroy replied that if French officers and men were to accept service under the British flag they would in law be guilty of desertion. To the second, that the ships should be demilitarized and immobilized, and so preserved unless the Germans or the Italians broke the armistice, in exchange for a British guarantee to pay and feed such of the ship's companies as chose to remain and to repatriate the others, he gave encouraging signs of probable agreement. To the third, that he should take his ships out and sink them, he naturally showed himself little disposed. Cunningham emphasized that his instructions required him to demand an answer by one o'clock and that the decision must be made by the admiral himself without reference to his government in Vichy. Godfroy, courteous and co-operative in his turn, promised an answer by half-past eleven. The time was then about half-past eight.

Cunningham signalled this hopeful result to the Admiralty, adding his own interpretation that at the back of his mind Godfroy was considering the possibility, perhaps the probability, that the Italians would infringe the terms of the armistice, thus freeing him to rejoin his British allies as a full combatant. Throughout the morning signals were coming in from Force H which indicated a most unpromising state of affairs. Was Admiral Gensoul at Oran keeping his colleague at Alexandria equally well-informed? Even if he wasn't it could only be a matter of minutes before the effects of an attack there would be felt throughout the active units of the French navy.

At noon came Godfroy's bitterly disappointing reply. He chose the third option, the sinking of his ships. The second, which he much preferred, was a decision that, on reflection, he felt he could only take if he were permitted to consult his own government. He asked for a delay of 48 hours to arrange for the disembarkation and transport of his crews. This Cunningham at once granted, sealing the understanding in the concluding sentence: 'I am therefore under the painful necessity of asking you to proceed to sea to carry out your purpose at 12.00 on Friday 5 July.'

Cunningham's own account of the agonizing dilemma in which he found himself is so succinct that it defies summary and so exact that it would only be blurred by paraphrase:

While this appeared to settle the question of the French squadron, most unsatisfactorily it is true, it did not satisfy the desire of the British Government that the squadron should be incapable of action by dark that night. We were also dissatisfied ['We' here means himself, Rear-Admiral Algernon Willis and Commander Royer Dick] that Godfroy had accepted the third choice, when he had so nearly accepted the second. To us it seemed certain that if his ships could be preserved in a demilitarized condition they would eventually rejoin us or fall into our hands. In either case they would not be lost to France. One more effort had therefore to be made to try and meet all these considerations. One of the principal stumbling blocks was the removal of the majority of the French crews.

So I wrote Godfroy a further letter, a private one to him personally, in which I said I had been casting round in my mind for some solution to this terrible impasse. I understood that he was primarily concerned with the fact that it was incompatible with his duty to remove the crews from his ships. Did not the solution lie in a compromise? If he could make a gesture, which indeed he had already offered to do, it would allow the British Government to realize that his ships would not proceed to sea, and that even now we might prevent a disaster as painful to myself as to him. Would he be prepared to give orders to remove the oil from his ships, and to take the warheads off the torpedoes? The question of the retention or otherwise of the crews could be discussed later . . .

It was a stroke of genius. Godfroy at once accepted both proposals and by 5.30 p.m. the French ships were discharging their fuel. Every move, including this last coup, was reported at once to the Admiralty in London. The incoming wireless traffic was far less heartening. Things were going badly at Oran. Finally it became plain that Somerville, to his own profound misgiving, had been forced to open fire. Cunningham's own reactions to the succeeding developments of that interminable day are again best rendered in the words he wrote in his autobiography eleven years later:

At 8.15 p.m. we received a signal from the Admiralty indicating that they were most dissatisfied with the efforts we had made up-to-date. It read: 'Admiralty note that oil fuel is being discharged by French ships. Reduction of crews, especially by ratings, should however begin at once by landing or transfer to merchant ships, before dark tonight. Do not, repeat NOT, fail.'

It is a perfect example of the type of signal which should never be made. Apart from being quite unhelpful, it showed no comprehension whatever of the explosive atmosphere at Alexandria or the difficult conditions in which we were working. It filled me with indignation. Moreover, while ordering us to take action before dark, it was sent off from the Admiralty at a time which was after sunset at Alexandria. As it was impossible to implement it we ignored it completely. At the time I did not believe that signal emanated in the Admiralty, and do not believe it now.

I assembled the Flag Officers on board the *Warspite* that evening and made them aware of the situation. I also told them it was not my intention to take action on this latest Admiralty signal, and was happy to find that all of them, without exception, were in complete agreement with me.

This passage will bear a little exposition. Perhaps no other so clearly exhibits and yet is so clearly anxious to play down its author's claim to greatness. When Cunningham emphasizes his certainty that Pound was not the true originator of the signal he means, of course, that Churchill was. And there and then, at a crucial moment of the war, he was ready to take the huge risk of flat disobedience to him.

> He either fears his fate too much
> Or his deserts are small
> That dares not put it to the touch
> To win or lose it all.

Few of Montrose's compatriots have shown so good a title to deserve the commendation implied. Comparison with Nelson at Copenhagen at once suggests itself. But to disregard the nervous twitterings of Sir Hyde Parker was one thing, to take on Churchill, in supreme and virtually uncontrolled power, quite another. In that terrible and utterly unpredictable situation a hundred things might go wrong: if only one did, Cunningham's head was on the block. He knew that Churchill had already expressed a lack of confidence in his fighting spirit. He was under no illusions as to that great man's unscrupulousness. 'He's a rascal but he's a great leader', as he wrote in a private letter a few months later (10 February 1941). It is characteristic of Cunningham in the final sentences of this passage to distract the reader's attention from the risk, the probability, of instant dismissal and disgrace that he had chosen to run by pointing to the loyalty and support of his subordinates. One can hardly wonder that so brave and generous a man should have commanded it.

The day was not over yet. Soon after the signal from London came a personal, handwritten letter from the French admiral. He had heard of the ultimatum issued by Somerville at Oran and had received a signal from his own admiralty ordering him to sail at once. He had replied, after querying the authenticity of the order, that sailing was for the moment impossible but had felt in honour bound to stop discharging his fuel. He added an explicit assurance that his intentions remained unchanged from those he had expressed in writing that morning. Given the circumstances this was more than might have been expected. But it wiped out the huge gains of the afternoon. What might happen when he heard that French ships had been fired on and Frenchmen killed?

Willis, the Chief of Staff, at once went aboard the French flagship. In a long interview Godfroy gave no ground. In fact he withdrew his original agreement to take his ships to sea and sink them in deep water. He would remain in harbour with his crews and his fuel aboard. If force were threatened he would scuttle his ships in harbour though he considerately promised to do so in the manner least obstructive to his British allies. The only thread of hope was precisely this: that both the French and the British admirals understood and respected the sense of honour in each other that exposed them to such intolerable strains. 'If you show a Frenchman that you do not trust to his "honeur" [sic] he just will not deal with you,' Cunningham wrote years later apropos the negotiations at

Oran. He knew what he was doing.

It was well into the small hours before the Commander-in-Chief retired to bed after reporting this latest turn in affairs to the Admiralty. Short of a battle in Alexandria harbour, the worst possible contingency, the only course of action seemed to be a demand for internment or surrender of the ships which would lead at once to their being scuttled.

Early the next morning even that dismal prospect had receded. During the night Godfroy had heard about the slaughter at Oran. Before seven he had sent a message disavowing all his previous undertakings. He would take his ships to sea, fighting his way out if he had to, without any limit to his subsequent freedom of action.

Cunningham at once went on deck. He could see for himself that the French ships were indeed raising steam and appeared to be clearing for action. The worst possible scenario, a battle in Alexandria harbour, now seemed inevitable. 'One chance only remained. I knew it would take the French ships six to eight hours to raise steam and be ready to move, so this short space of time was vouchsafed to us to take what measures we could to induce Vice-Admiral Godfroy to see reason. We decided to appeal to his officers and ships' companies over his head and suborn them from their allegiance to him. It was a most distasteful task; but the only possible thing to do.'

Cunningham goes on in his autobiography to describe the methods he employed to communicate the facts of the situation to each ship, by signal, by personal visits by individual captains and liaison officers, even, as in the mutinies of 1797, by chalking the message on large blackboards and taking them round in boats. Strangely he does not mention what was probably the most effective stroke of all. Godfroy had broken off all communication with his British colleague: but Cunningham's Flag Lieutenant reminded Commander Royer Dick that the *Warspite* was still linked to the French flagship by telephone. Commander Dick at once rang up his friend Auboyneau and a substantial basis of agreement was established with Godfroy's own staff officers. Soon the captains of other French ships could be seen coming alongside the flagship while large numbers of their ship's companies could be seen gathering on the forecastles. It began to look as if a bloodless solution were after all possible.

Meanwhile the Admiralty was profuse in impracticable advice, of which the silliest recommendation is printed by Stephen Roskill, not by Cunningham: namely, that he should lead the British fleet out of harbour and take up position to fight the French when they were well clear of the shore installations, depot ships and all the paraphernalia on which the maintenance of an effective fighting force depended. Why the French should steam obediently out like lambs to the slaughter leaving all this untouched behind them was not explained.

Fortunately Godfroy retained a firmer grip on his senses. He recognized that his position had crumbled, asked for an interview with Cunningham and yielded to overwhelming force. All remaining oil fuel was to be discharged at once and the ships were to be rendered incapable of fighting. 'Never in my life', wrote the Admiral looking back, 'have I experienced such a whole-hearted feeling of thankful relief as on the conclusion of this agreement.' The First Lord and First Sea Lord, perhaps somewhat ashamed of the insulting signal they had authorized, were generous in their recognition both of what the Commander-in-Chief had been through and what he had achieved: 'After what must have been a most trying and anxious time your negotiations have achieved complete success. We offer you our most sincere congratulations. The Prime Minister also wishes his congratulations to be sent to you.'

The coolness of this concluding accolade was doubtless not lost on its recipient. Cunningham's success at Alexandria set Churchill's action at Oran in a different moral and political perspective from that in which he wished it to be viewed. 'Winston never forgave A.B.C. for Alexandria,' was the judgement of Admiral Royer Dick who, in his later appointments as he rose in seniority on Cunningham's staff, was well placed to observe the relations of these two great men.

Cunningham has recorded his own strongly expressed opposition to the proposed, and subsequently executed, action at Oran. From this he never deviated. On 9 January 1950 he wrote to the then First Sea Lord '90% of senior naval officers, including myself, thought Oran a ghastly error and still do.' As the official historian of *The War at Sea* has written: 'While working on my war history I had many interviews and much correspondence with Cunningham, Somerville and North, the three admirals concerned in the execution of the attack on Oran and related plans. None of them ever budged from the view that, given more time for negotiation, the tragedy could have been averted.'

The importance of this unanimity of the commanders on the spot is that it isolates the responsibility of Mr Churchill in going against their clear and strong advice. The credit or the shame of the action is his and his alone. No statesman of our century had a more vivid sense of history or showed a greater readiness to appeal to its verdict. 'Nearly all my work has been done in writing, and a complete record exists of all the directions I have given, the inquiries I have made, and the telegrams I have drafted. I shall be perfectly content to be judged by them.' These words, taken from his reply to a censure motion in July 1942, are as effective against his posthumous denigrators as they were against the parliamentary pygmy who then assailed him.

But the essence of an appeal to history is that it is an appeal against verdict, not against sentence. And if the throwing out of a hostile verdict is sought, the discrediting of hostile witnesses is implicit in the process. Churchill's subsequent treatment of Admiral North can hardly be cited by his most fervent admirers as an instance of his magnanimity or even of his fair-mindedness. His attempt to discredit Somerville, to which Cunningham objected at once and in the most forthright terms, led, as we shall see, to the scoring of an own goal. Cunningham himself, whose opposition to the Prime Minister had been crowned with a military as well as a moral success too plain to be denied, was, in the courtroom of history, the most dangerous witness of the three. It is perhaps significant that Mr Martin Gilbert in his biography of Churchill, a work that cannot be criticized for thinness of treatment or hastiness of research, does not so much as mention Cunningham's name in the chapter he devoted to Oran and the general question of the French navy. The reader collects that there was a sizable French force at Alexandria but the telescoping of information in a narrative of such generally awe-inspiring proportions leaves him with no clear idea of what happened there and why.

The more the question of the British action at Oran is studied in the light of evidence from all sides the more Cunningham's patience, firmness, clarity of mind and coolness of courage are to be admired. On both sides at Oran there was tragic muddle and misunderstanding. Gensoul, the French admiral, misreported to his own admiralty the terms that were offered. Darlan allowed the French attitude to appear more intransigent than it was. The War Cabinet in London rejected a draft signal from the First Sea Lord to Somerville which would in effect have authorized terms that Gensoul was ready to accept. The truisms about the wastefulness and wantonness of war are all too obvious. Martin Gilbert compares the killing of 1,250 French officers and men at Oran with the loss of nearly 800 lives the day before when a U-boat torpedoed the *Arandora Star*, a vessel carrying German and Italian internees and prisoners of war to Canada.

From the military point of view the comparison is neither here nor there. The U-boat captain was acting with the defiance of international law that had been enjoined on him and his brother officers from the start of the war and which the Allies were themselves driven to adopt. Oran, whatever may be thought of the causes and conduct of British policy, was another matter. The killing in cold blood of men who surrender in operations where the taking of prisoners has been forbidden is repugnant enough. But they have till that moment been in arms against you. Firing on your companions-in-arms has a depth of horror that cannot be sounded. 'If there was a stain on the flag that day it was not on ours,' wrote

Admiral Gensoul in his own post-war retrospect. Cunningham and Somerville accepted the same code of military honour. If they felt anger and resentment it may well have been because their consciences were being forced at the same time as their professional judgement as to the risks and probable results of a naval operation which they were called on to direct was being overridden. If Winston never forgave A.B.C. for Alexandria it is highly probable that A.B.C. harboured some strong feelings about Winston on the same account.

It is characteristic of Cunningham that he should conclude his own story of these unforgettable transactions with a measured, but generously measured, assessment of Godfroy. 'Placed in an unprecedented and most difficult situation, [he] conducted himself as an honourable if obstinate man. In the long and weary months that were to follow he remained on board his flagship and seldom went ashore. The fate of France and the tragedy of Mers-el-Kebir [the fleet anchorage at Oran] were always in his mind; but no success of the British fleet passed without his letter of cordial congratulation, no loss without his letter of sympathy.' He quotes such a letter, written in May 1941, just after the evacuation of Greece when things looked their blackest for Britain: 'Since we cannot fire our guns during these bombing attacks, we are reduced to watch. It is a pity we can do nothing, because our excellent stereoscopic range-finders would be very valuable at night . . . My thoughts were with you during all these last days we have passed . . . I try to remain patient . . . The idea of your understanding so well our situation helps me.' The last sentence flashes a glimpse of Cunningham's greatness.

The settlement of the French problem set Cunningham free to take the offensive against Italy. The key to all such operations was the retention of Malta, doubly vulnerable through its proximity to Sicilian airfields and through its dependence, in normal times, on Sicily and Southern Italy for its food. One of the most densely populated areas in Europe it was already, within weeks of the outbreak of war, beginning to run short. The first necessity was therefore to take out everyone who was willing to come before the siege tightened. So large an operation was certain to attract the attention of the Italian fleet. It would therefore have to be covered by Cunningham's main force.

The fleet sailed late in the evening of 7 July, a mere three days after the prolonged and acute anxieties of the business with the French. Leaving harbour at night was the almost invariable precaution to any large-scale operation since a large number of Egyptians, from the King downwards, were known to be pro-Axis. The fleet, on which the whole position in the near East depended, was a slender one for such responsibilities: three old battleships of the Jacky Fisher era of which only the famous *Warspite* had been modernized, so that at least she was not outranged, even if she was outpaced, by her Italian adversaries: one aging aircraft-carrier, HMS *Eagle*, five modern cruisers and seventeen destroyers.

But it was not the odds in surface vessels that were to test the Commander-in-Chief's courage and skill so much as the ample and unchallenged enemy supremacy in the air. Cunningham wrote:

> In all, during our five days at sea on this occasion, the *Warspite* and the five destroyers with her were attacked thirty-four times in four days . . . Particularly do I remember a most virulent attack on 12 July during our return passage to Alexandria when twenty-four heavy bombs fell along the port side of the ship simultaneously, with another dozen on our starboard bow, all within two hundred yards, but slightly out for line. It is not too much to say that the Italian high-level bombing was the best I have ever seen, far better than the German. Later, when our anti-aircraft fire improved and the trained squadrons of the Regia Aeronautica came to be knocked about by our fleet-fighters, their air work over the sea deteriorated. But I shall always remember it with respect. There was some consolation in realizing that there was always more water than ship. Nevertheless one felt very naked and unprotected.

On the morning after they left harbour the Admiral at Malta

reported a sighting of two Italian battleships and their escorts 200 miles to the east of the island on a southerly course. Cunningham concluded that they were covering an important convoy to Libya and, postponing his original operation, altered course towards Taranto so as to place himself between the enemy fleet and its base. Early the next morning, the 9th, a flying-boat from Malta reported the enemy fleet, consisting of two battleships, six cruisers and seven destroyers, 145 miles to the west of him. By noon the distance was down to 90 miles and closing rapidly. Just before 3 p.m. the English cruisers sighted the enemy escort. A few minutes later the cruiser *Neptune* 'sighted the Italian heavy ships, and was the first British warship to signal "Enemy battle fleet in sight" in the Mediterranean since the time of Nelson.' The Italian cruisers were eight-inch, the British six-inch. One British cruiser had been partly disabled by air attack the day before so that even in numbers it was four against six. The battleships *Malaya* and *Royal Sovereign* lumbering along in the rear could not help to redress the balance, so the *Warspite* pushed on with her destroyers. In the action that followed the shooting on both sides was very accurate so that it was just as well that the *Warspite* scored a direct hit on one of the battleships, causing the Italians to break off the action and turn away behind a smoke-screen. Close as the British fleet was to the Italian coast – some 30 miles or so – and slow as was the battle squadron, Cunningham worked round to windward of the smoke but to no effect. Cunningham wrote to his aunt a few days later: 'You will have seen that my old friend Riccardi, the Italian admiral who dined with me 3 years ago in Hood, came out and had a look at us. He didn't like what he saw as he left the neighbourhood at some speed . . . a disappointing affair but you can't catch ships that go 7 knots faster than you do.'

Cunningham never overvalued his own performance. But he was surely right when he wrote a decade later: 'The one 15-inch hit they sustained from the *Warspite* had a moral effect quite out of proportion to the damage. Never again did they willingly face up to the fire of British battleships, though on several subsequent occasions they were in a position to give battle with a great preponderance in force.' To have seized that advantage when the forces of the Crown had suffered, and were still to suffer, defeat after defeat was not the least of his achievements.

The convoy from Malta that the fleet had put to sea to cover had escaped the attentions of the Italians and arrived safely in Alexandria. From this moment to the end of his time as Commander-in-Chief the supply of Malta and its effective use as a base against the troop traffic to North Africa was Cunningham's constant preoccupation. Whether it was a question of supporting Wavell's brilliant offensive or denying Rommel the oil that kept his armour rumbling forward and the high-octane spirit needed for his fighters and dive-bombers, Malta was beyond price. The consequences of its loss did not bear thinking about.

This first brush with the Italians defined the principal deficiencies of the Mediterranean fleet. The capital ships were too slow and too apt to require docking, a facility for which Alexandria was poorly equipped and dangerously vulnerable to air attack. The supply of ammunition was low. There was no depot ship for the destroyers to answer their myriad occasions. There were no anti-aircraft cruisers for fleet or convoy escort. A modern carrier with an armoured flight-deck was essential if the fleet was not to be harried by constant air attack every time it put to sea. RAF cover from shore bases was of course out of the question when the Battle of Britain itself still hung in the balance.

It is a tribute to Dudley Pound's management of the Admiralty that so many of these necessities were so rapidly supplied at a period when, only a few weeks earlier, the government had been weighing the pros and cons of a total withdrawal from the Eastern Mediterranean. Cunningham took advantage of the moonless nights of August to dock two of his battleships and devoted a great deal of his time to conferring with his fellow Commanders-in-Chief in Cairo, Wavell and Longmore, with both of whom he enjoyed the happiest relations. Their forces were even smaller than his own and an Italian offensive in the Western Desert was known to be imminent. His offer of a naval bombardment of the advanced posts and bases was gratefully accepted and successfully executed. Otherwise there was no fleet action. The Australian cruiser *Sydney* distinguished herself by taking on two heavier opponents, sinking one and damaging the other. The brilliance of the action was enhanced by the humanity of her Captain who brought over 500 survivors into Alexandria though heavily attacked from the air. Two months later Cunningham was censured by the Admiralty for signalling in plain language to the Italian admiralty the position of survivors on rafts dropped by a British destroyer that had been deterred from picking them up by the approach of enemy aircraft. He was to do exactly the same after his victory off Matapan the following year.

At the end of August the fleet sailed to meet the reinforcements, sent through the Western Mediterranean under the protection of Force H, and to run a convoy into Malta at the same time. The Italians were known to have mined the Sicilian narrows extensively but the position of the minefields was anyone's guess. The nightmare that haunted the Commander-in-Chief was a badly damaged battleship with no means of repairing her. The operation was however successful and the fleet was strengthened by another middle-aged battleship, two anti-aircraft cruisers and, best of all, a modern fleet aircraft-carrier.

To naval commanders capital ships appear in the light that major pieces do to a chess-player. Essentially their function is to support or to threaten. To have them whistling up and down the board is to expose them to risks disproportionate to their military value. By Mr Churchill they seem to have been regarded as high-fed hunters that ought to be out with the hounds, not snorting and stamping in the stable. He accordingly accompanied these reinforcements with an admonition to the Commander-in-Chief to step up his offensive operations against the Italians. Cunningham was not prepared to be taught his job by a politician, however brilliant, who had no first-hand experience of fighting at sea and only the briefest of soldiering at a very junior level. No doubt he felt personally insulted at the implication that he had not been as ready as he might have been to engage the enemy. And he made it quite clear in a stiff reply that until more destroyers were available it was impossible both to escort the convoys urgently demanded and to screen the battle fleet. It was, obviously, the Commander-in-Chief's responsibility to decide the priorities at any given moment. In fact for the rest of his time each convoy to Malta – and there were generally two a month – became a fleet operation.

In mid-September the Italian army crossed the Egyptian frontier but to everyone's surprise halted their offensive. The fleet could not do much beyond occasional bombardment. But at the end of October the Italian declaration of war on Greece widened the area of naval responsibility. Nothing much happened at first but sooner or later convoys of troops and equipment would have to be run. In the meantime the supply of Malta and the bombing of Alexandria took a steady toll of ships though the Italians never got the best of it when it came to a surface action.

Early in November Cunningham took the fleet to sea for what was to prove the most spectacular and the least costly of all his victories. The attack on the Italian fleet in the harbour of Taranto has been too often and too well described for any narration to be necessary. Three Italian battleships were sunk at the cost of two aircraft and four lives. Not until the Americans after a grimly fought battle sank four Japanese carriers at Midway was so sudden and dramatic a change in the balance of power achieved by the allies in any theatre. It was a victory on the grand scale. Cunningham had originally planned it for Trafalgar Day but had had to postpone it on account of an accident in the carrier *Illustrious*. In the proportion of ships sunk or damaged on the two sides it came nearer to the Battle of the Nile.

The planning of the operation had been as skilful as its execution. A diversionary attack on the sea communications with Albania across the Straits of Otranto had been successful in its primary purpose as well as in its incidental effect. Of a convoy of four merchant ships three were sunk. Taranto opened a sudden period of brilliant success for British arms. A month later Wavell with grotesquely inferior forces defeated his Italian opponents, overran Cyrenaica and captured enormous numbers of prisoners. But it was Taranto that had shown the world that Britain could still win victories.

Among the congratulations that were showered on him, Cunningham quotes with particular pleasure those of the King. He does not mention Churchill's, which were in fact warm. Might he have been on the way to forgiving Cunningham for having proved himself so resoundingly right about Alexandria? Magnanimity as well as vindictiveness are both conspicuous features of the Churchillian landscape. Two causes of contention unhappily blighted this possibility, if possibility it was. Both arose from Churchill's relations with two admirals, each intimately known to Cunningham.

The first, which involved the First Lord and, apparently, the First Sea Lord as well as Churchill himself, was the disgraceful treatment of Cunningham's old term-mate and fellow Commander-in-Chief, James Somerville. Towards the end of November Force H had been ordered to cover a small but exceptionally important convoy of three fast merchantmen, two bound for Malta and one for Alexandria. Off the southern tip of Sardinia a powerful Italian squadron was encountered which immediately retreated. Somerville set off in hot pursuit but, as usual, the Italian ships were much faster and quickly drew out of range. Somerville who had broken radio silence to report his giving chase signalled his abandonment of it. He could not catch the enemy: the protection of the convoy was the duty with which he had been charged. On the strength of these two signals, without waiting for the admiral to return to harbour and make his report, the Admiralty at once appointed a Court of Enquiry under Admiral of the Fleet Lord Cork, whom Somerville found waiting for him at Gibraltar when he returned from the successful completion of his mission. Cunningham was outraged by this gratuitous public display of want of confidence in a commander and by the injustice of not letting him explain his conduct before so censuring him. He expressed his views with some vigour in a personal letter to Pound, who had himself played a less than heroic part in these proceedings. Had Cunningham known of First Lord of the Admiralty A. V. Alexander's action in nominating Somerville's relief before the Court had even taken evidence and of Churchill's approving minute, clearly identifying Somerville's reluctance to fire on the French at Oran as one of the reasons for doubting his 'offensive spirit', he would have been angrier still. In the event the Court, once it had heard Somerville's report, completely exonerated him and approved his action.

The second embroiled Cunningham more directly. This was the plan, originated by Sir Roger Keyes and enthusiastically backed by Churchill, for the capture of Pantellaria, the diminutive and militarily useless island in the narrows between Sicily and Tunisia. Keyes, whose fighting spirit Cunningham had always admired, had been brought out of retirement by Churchill and appointed to the new post of Director of Combined Operations in July 1940. The concept of the commandos and the choice of Keyes to form them perfectly exemplified Churchill's magnificent, electrifying determination to go on to the offensive that transformed the direction of the war. The appointment, however, turned out to be a mistake. Keyes for all his great qualities of energy and dash and his first-hand experience of the hazards of attacking from sea was quarrelsome, difficult and egotistic. He was also immensely senior – an Admiral of the Fleet of ten years' standing. Years ago Pound, now First Sea Lord, had been his Flag Captain. Keyes soon made it plain that he considered the Chiefs of Staff Committee a timorous body of professional obstructionists and had no hesitation in writing to the Prime Minister direct, sometimes in terms so violent that Churchill had to refuse to receive his letters.

It was in October that Keyes responded enthusiastically to Churchill's question whether Pantellaria could be captured. In November the Chiefs of Staff reported somewhat tepidly on the project. But a few days later in the middle of an air raid Keyes was brought in an armoured car to a late night meeting over which

Churchill himself presided. Churchill expounded Keyes's plan, overrode all objections and ended by emphasizing to Keyes that he would be given the actual command of the operation (henceforth code-named 'Workshop'). A week later Churchill confirmed this, even adding that Keyes would not, as he expected, have to take a step or two down in rank but would serve as an Admiral of the Fleet. He would thus outrank the Commander-in-Chief Mediterranean.

Pound, on this occasion, was not on the Prime Minister's side of the fence. He thought the project ill-conceived and strategically valueless and he was alarmed at the idea of Keyes conducting an independent naval war with private lines of communication to the Prime Minister. He wisely concealed his reservations, guessing, correctly, that the scheme would almost certainly be overtaken by events. He made sure however that Cunningham was fully informed as to what was in the wind. A.B.C.'s reactions are forcefully stated in his autobiography:

> I considered it a wild-cat scheme. I had no doubt at all that the island could easily be captured, and held afterwards. But I was frankly aghast at the notion of adding to our already heavy commitments another island in a position more or less dominated by the enemy. We were having difficulty enough in maintaining Malta. To add to it Pantellaria with a garrison and its considerable civil population seemed to me to be the height of unwisdom. Nor could I see what possible use Pantellaria would be to us.

There was, he points out, no harbour worthy of the name: the small airfield would have to be supplied with base facilities and stores: and there was no fresh water.

With the quiet support of the Chiefs of Staff Committee he succeeded in having the operation postponed in November. Early in December he replied to a personal signal from Churchill:

> I have never questioned the feasibility of Workshop given

thorough planning but my concern has always lain in its subsequent maintenance.

The hard fact is that my resources are strained beyond their limits already and the extra burden means that something else will have to suffer in consequence . . . The calls on my forces increase almost daily, for instance to-day I am arranging for the supply of the Army in the Western Desert and for the removal by sea of some 20,000 prisoners . . .

In a later paragraph he added, without referring to Keyes by name: 'The organisation for command appears likely to lead to awkward and unsatisfactory situations.'

Churchill never liked being stood up to by subordinates, especially if they were admirals. Such plain speaking might well have lit the touch paper of a thunderbolt. But the unforeseen rapidity of Wavell's advance swept Workshop aside: on New Year's Eve, to Keyes's fury, the operation was postponed for two months. In effect it was the end of it.

The ghost of Jacky Fisher might have been discerned in its shadow. Keyes never lost an opportunity of reminding Churchill that he alone among the senior naval officers at Gallipoli had dissented from Fisher and had continued to insist that the Straits could be forced by naval assault alone. Here was history repeating itself. The timid, desk-bound Committees of Brass Hats were once again preventing the natural, inspired warriors like Churchill and himself from seizing an enemy stronghold, this time commanding the Straits of the Central, rather than the Eastern, Mediterranean. Keyes knew his man. There was a seasoning of nostalgic allusions to their shared prowess on the polo field, transcending the constipated life-style of the Whitehall bureaucracy that obstructed them. And bold defiance of advancing age struck another sympathetic note:

St Vincent was at his zenith as First Sea Lord when he was older than I am now, and hoisted his Flag again after that.

I am younger than Howe was on his Glorious First of June and

I don't suppose either of them possessed such a spare and healthy body.

Winston – back me in this and you will never regret it.[33]

Although Workshop had been scuppered, Keyes was still going strong. In a letter to the Prime Minister more than faintly echoing Fisher's ultimatum to Asquith he suggested that he should be made First Sea Lord or even, while he was about it, First Lord: 'As First Lord, I could have a Labour Under Secretary. That ought to satisfy the Labour Party and surely something might be found for Alexander more in keeping with his outlook and capabilities.' Churchill rejected the letter; but so far from sacking its writer sent, a few days later, a rebuke to Cunningham for having written in a personal letter to Pound that he did not welcome the idea of Keyes arriving on his station in an independent command.

Was Cunningham inconsistent in his opinions of Keyes? 'In Man, the judgement shoots at flying game.' The brief *éloge* in *A Sailor's Odyssey* is just and generous: 'a great figure who did a lot for the Navy'. As First Sea Lord at the time of Keyes's death he had to withstand an all-out effort by his widow to have him buried with Nelson in St Paul's. 'It is not easy to tell a bereaved lady that her husband was not really in the class that gets buried in the national cathedral,' he wrote in his diary. 'Roger was in many ways a fine man, in some ways a great man. He was not much good as C o S to de Robeck at the Dardanelles but he had an offensive spirit which at times undoubtedly clouded his judgement. At Dover he was good, but there again he rather spoiled things by being a bit frightened of his reputation.

'He did not increase his stature by his political activities and certainly in this war as Chief of Combined Operations he was a nuisance . . .'

The discrimination of this judgement is as evident as its candour and its generosity. The courtesy that Cunningham, at a time of extreme pressure, showed to his old commanding officer is strikingly revealed in this letter written in his own hand on 10

March 1941.

I think my reply [to a letter from Keyes of which he had just received a duplicate] went down with the *Hyperion* when she was mined off Pantellaria.

In it I gave you my reasons for opposing 'Workshop'. *The chief one being* the difficulty of supply after capture.

I am very glad it did not take place. I think it would have been a disaster, the whole sea that morning was alive with German dive-bombers & as you know the *Illustrious* was badly knocked about so I don't suppose the 'Glen' ships [the four fast liners converted for landing troops] would have lasted very long. Further we are having enough difficulty at the moment in supplying Malta without having to supply an Island 150 miles beyond . . .

The Lofoten affair [the Commando raid in the Lofoten islands] judging by the press appears to have been a good show. I suppose some of your experts were in it.

All best wishes & please forgive me for not tumbling to the fact that your answer was sunk sooner . . .

As this letter indicates January 1941, the month for which Workshop had been scheduled, had seen the war in the Mediterranean take a deadlier turn. The arrival of the German dive-bombers in Sicily put an immediate end to such limited protection from air attack as the fleet had enjoyed since *Illustrious* had joined it. On 10 January Cunningham had watched with admiration the skill and precision of the German pilots:

The attacks were pressed home to point-blank range, and as they pulled out of their dives some of them were seen to fly along the flight-deck of the *Illustrious* below the level of her funnel.

I saw her hit early on just before the bridge, and in all, in something like ten minutes, she was hit by six 1,000 lb bombs, to leave the line badly on fire, her steering gear crippled, her lifts out of action, with heavy casualties . . .

Her aircraft were able to land in Malta, to which she struggled in for temporary repairs. After an anxious fortnight in which the German air force was able to attack more or less continuously and with very little opposition from fighters she got away to Alexandria. This was a tribute to her designers and to the coolness and courage of the naval constructors in Malta, working round the clock often under heavy attack. But it did nothing to ease the burdens on the fleet. On the contrary it increased them. Until she could be got away through the canal for repairs in America she was a liability. German aircraft were now mining the canal, the blocking of which either by sabotage or the sinking of a large vessel in passage was one of the constant anxieties of the Commander-in-Chief. The *Formidable*, which was sent out to relieve her, was only able to clear a wreck in the canal by a few feet. Until she berthed in Alexandria on 10 March, two months to the day since *Illustrious* had been hit, the fleet was without air cover. And *Formidable* had only recently commissioned and finished working up.

The early months of 1941 were to see the fiercest and most bloody battles in the history of the Royal Navy since the Dutch wars of the late seventeenth century. In Cunningham's war the German superiority in the air was absolute. Time after time he had to send his ships out to take what he knew, none better, would be terrible punishment for gains which were at best negative or which opened only a perspective of further sacrifice. There were battles in the Dutch wars that must have looked like that to the English commanders. One thinks of Monck in the Battle of the Four Days, leading out an inferior force each morning against a resolute, well found and skilfully commanded enemy. Cunningham no doubt drew more inspiration from Nelson; he knew more about him and had, quite naturally, been more exposed to him in the naval climate of his day. The theatre in which he was serving was one that Nelson had made his own. But his situation and the military qualities it demanded, doggedness, resolution, tenacity, seem closer to Monck's.

The arrival of the Luftwaffe was correctly interpreted as the beginning of full-scale German intervention in the Mediterranean. Greece who had been confident of dealing with the Italians on her own now asked for British reinforcements. Throughout March convoys were run to the Piraeus carrying British troops and equipment drawn from Wavell's none too numerous force. The RAF too sent squadrons that could ill be spared. The British position in Libya was thus dangerously weak; the lines of communication that supported it were long and glaringly exposed to enemy air attack; Malta which ought to have been a springboard for counter-offensive was still unable to defend her magnificent harbour and base installations from incessant bombing. Naval commitments, already huge, were still increasing. On 1 March the Germans entered Bulgaria. The attack on Greece could not be long delayed.

Cunningham's first act on being reinforced by *Formidable* was to take the battle fleet to sea to cover a Malta convoy. This was achieved without loss and the fleet was back in Alexandria late on 24 March. Within 48 hours the Italians had carried out one of those brilliant and daring operations against a fleet at which they excelled. Six fast explosive motor-boats entered the harbour early in the morning of the 26th and put the heavy cruiser *York*, the only eight-inch cruiser on the station, out of action for several weeks. Next day every vessel that could take part in a fleet action was put at short notice for steam as an air sighting from Malta reported strong Italian forces on a course that suggested an attack on the lightly defended Greek convoys. The fleet left Alexandria late on the 27th, with the object of placing itself between the Italian forces and the one convoy bound for the Piraeus which happened to be at sea.

Early the next morning the *Formidable*'s aircraft reported four Italian cruisers close to the position of the British cruisers that were screening the convoy. The Italian cruisers were, as Cunningham expected, supported by a battleship which opened an accurate fire at a range of sixteen miles. Her superior speed enabled her to shorten it as the British turned and ran for it, intending to draw her towards Cunningham's powerful but painfully slow battle squadron. To protect the cruisers which were still unable to return an unpleasantly well-directed fire Cunningham flew off an air-strike from *Formidable*. This achieved its immediate object but had the undesired effect of inducing the battleship, the *Vittorio Veneto*, to turn for home after she had suffered a hit that somewhat reduced her speed.

Encouraged by optimistic reports of this reduction the British fleet made its best speed in pursuit. But by early evening it was clear that they were not going to catch her before dark, if at all. Every mile they laid off brought them closer to the enemy airfields. Was it worth exposing the fleet on which so much depended to a day's target-practice by the Luftwaffe in the hopes of intercepting the *Vittorio Veneto* next morning? Cunningham's staff officers on the whole thought not. He reflected on their arguments over his solitary evening meal and decided not to accept them. 'I hate staff officers who agree with me,' were the first words that he had addressed to Commander Manley Power (subsequently a distinguished admiral) on taking up his appointment. As the fleet steamed on through the darkness another sharp-eyed staff officer on *Warspite*'s bridge sighted three cruisers about to cross the British course from starboard. Commander Power, an ex-submariner, at once identified them as two eight-inch and one light Italian cruisers. *Warspite*, *Valiant* and *Barham* opened fire at point-blank range. The enemy, caught unawares, had no chance of reply. After a few minutes of inferno the Battle of Matapan was over.

Torpedo attacks by the Italian destroyers that had been escorting the cruiser squadron were evaded and the British destroyer escort fought a successful if confused action with them while the fleet withdrew. The great hazard of a night action is mistaking one's own forces for the enemy. Cunningham himself intervened in the nick of time to save the *Formidable* (in which my brother was serving) from a sixteen-inch salvo from *Warspite*. In his own account of the battle written in retirement he both criticizes his own conduct of operations during the night and reflects, fairly, on the distinction between hindsight and real life: 'Instant and momentous decisions have to be made in a matter of seconds. With fast-moving ships at close quarters and the roar of heavy gunfire, clear thinking is not easy.' Michael Culme-Seymour who was with him on the bridge when the Italian cruisers were sighted remembers his instantaneous ordering of *Formidable* out of the line. An aircraft-carrier is the most vulnerable of all targets and useless in a night action.

Perfectionism is beside the point. Never was a naval victory more desperately needed or more thirstily received. For months there had been nothing but putting to sea in the sure knowledge of savage, unopposed air attack. In the weeks that were to follow, the carnage and the sinkings were to reduce a great fleet to a battered remnant. Cruisers were to sail with their bows blown off and patched-up, or with only one of their two propellers working. Destroyers were rarely to spend more than twelve hours in harbour. Officers and men were to be tried up to and beyond breaking-point. In all this Cunningham was to show an adamantine resolution, a leadership that neither faltered nor would countenance faltering. Its moral quality was enhanced by the absence of joy in battle such as Churchill certainly felt. Cunningham's imagination, his humanity and his own direct experience of the hideousness of war kept him only too well aware of the horrors he was committing his men to face. Two years later Royer Dick who had rejoined his staff in North Africa remembers him coming and sitting on the end of his bed, unable to undress and go to sleep for the thought of what was happening to the men he had sent into battle.

Within ten days of Matapan blows were raining on every position in the Central and Eastern Mediterranean. Germany had invaded Yugoslavia and Greece and it rapidly became clear to the Commanders on the spot that evacuation rather than reinforcement of British troops in Greece would soon be imperative. At the same time the weakened army in the Western Desert was being swept back, its armour lost, its generals captured. It even became a question whether Tobruk could be held. Cunningham gave it as his opinion that it could be supplied from the sea. 'Had I been gifted with second sight and been able to foresee the long tale of ships lost and damaged in supplying the fortress, I very much doubt if I should have been so confident in saying that it could be done.'

Malta was still in Cunningham's view the great unexploited resource. If only adequate air cover were provided Malta could turn the tables on the enemy. Air reconnaissance could report the movements of convoys from Italy to Libya and the submarines based in Malta could sink them. Even as things were the submarines were achieving marvels: but their losses were high and unopposed bombing of the base made rest for the crews and repairs to the boats increasingly difficult. The priority given by the government to the bombing of Germany was to exact a high price from the navy in the Mediterranean and in the Atlantic. But far from answering Cunningham's repeated requests for substantial reinforcements of the RAF specifically committed to providing fighter protection and long range reconnaissance, the signals he received assured him that Air Ministry statistics showed an ample force in the Middle East and impressed on him the importance of reinforcing first Greece and then Crete when it was already plain to him as to Wavell that those battles had been lost beyond any hope.

The naval casualties of those operations in confined waters, without any facilities for disembarking troops or re-embarking them, without a scintilla of air defence against a seemingly ceaseless storm of attack, were appalling. April and May were indeed comparable, on a still larger scale, to the Four Days Battle of June 1666. There was no rest for the ships of the Royal Navy until they were crippled or sunk. In return for this there were some tangible achievements. In a brilliant destroyer action based on Malta a whole enemy convoy of five large ships together with their escort was destroyed. Early in May the fleet sailed out to meet a through-Mediterranean convoy carrying tanks to replace the losses in the desert. The operation also included the cover of convoys to and from Malta. Earlier, in April, the fleet had made a special sortie for the bombardment of Tripoli, the great harbour on the North African coast. All these objectives were achieved without serious loss, more, in Cunningham's opinion, by luck than by judgement.

For once in May unseasonable cloud-cover in the central Mediterranean protected the battle fleet from the air forces for which, unsupported, it was no match.

Cunningham had advised against sending the tank convoy through the Mediterranean instead of round the Cape, but accepted the decision as a gamble worth taking. The bombardment of Tripoli he thought a risk disproportionate to any advantage to be obtained from its success. 'It had taken the whole Mediterranean Fleet five days to accomplish what a heavy bomber squadron working from Egypt could probably carry out in a few hours. The fleet had also to run considerable, and in my opinion, unjustifiable risks in an operation which had been carried out at the expense of all other commitments, when those commitments were most pressing.' The evacuation of Greece in which the navy brought out 50,000 soldiers operating several hundred miles from its nearest base and under constant attack was imminent; the reinforcement of Crete urgent; the requirements of Tobruk pressing; the needs of Malta perpetual.

The Commander-in-Chief had put up a stiff fight against the Tripoli venture. But he had put up a stiffer, and ultimately successful, resistance to a far more wild and wasteful project on which the Prime Minister had set his heart, that of blocking the entrance to Tripoli harbour by sinking the battleship *Barham* and a cruiser in its mouth. The scheme like so many Churchillian projects for the use of sea-power owed more to the Prime Minister's recollection of picturesque incidents from the First World War and perhaps to his friendship with Keyes than to any consideration of how a warship worked and what its functions might be, still less to those of geography or strategy or the history of maritime warfare. In all these matters Cunningham was, and knew himself to be, better equipped than his master.

The technical objections he put forward were overwhelming. Even were the enemy to turn a blind eye to the whole proceeding it would be a navigational feat of the nicest delicacy to manoeuvre a battleship drawing 32 feet of water, leaving a mere 2 feet under her keel, into the exact position where she could wedge herself so as to seal the channel. Under point-blank fire from the heavy guns defending the harbour, to say nothing of the attentions of the dive-bombers from an airfield only a couple of minutes away, the idea was grotesque. Even were the impossible achieved and the *Barham* sunk, by her own act or as an effect of enemy attack, in the desired position the port would still not be closed since unloading into lighters within the reefs that protected the anchorage would be perfectly practicable: indeed it was already in practice.

But it was not the tactical hazard or the strategical imbecility of the scheme that disturbed him most deeply. Once again, as at Alexandria, it was the human and the moral. By long tradition in the navy, operations involving the deliberate destruction of one of HM ships were undertaken by volunteer crews, fully aware of the risks and purposes of the enterprise and provided with some means, however improbable, of avoiding the fate of their vessel. Such had been the procedure in manning the fire-ships that had been used with such success in the sixteenth and seventeenth centuries. The precedent had been followed by Keyes in 1918 and indeed by Cunningham himself when he was chosen by Keyes to command the old battleship *Swiftsure* to block the entrance to Ostend in the same year. That operation had been called off at the last moment, to Cunningham's intense disappointment. But he retained vivid memories of the excitement with which he and his ship's company had prepared for it.

What was now proposed was a very different application of military morals. Risks, of death, of mutilation and other horrors, are obviously implicit in all military activity, and a commander has both the duty and the right to expose his men to them. But what when risk gives way to certainty? Cunningham steeled himself during the evacuation of Greece and Crete to send his ships out to face what might be thought the virtual certainty of heavy loss and dreadful casualties. But the certainty was not absolute and the losses were not, emphatically not, planned by his own staff. The risks, as he better than any critic could appreciate, were desperate.

But so was the situation he had to relieve. To abandon British soldiers to their fate when there was still a chance of bringing them back to take their part in the war was unacceptable. The saying attributed to him at this time, 'It takes two years to build a warship: it takes two hundred to build a naval tradition', referred directly to the obligation of the navy to support its sister service to the utmost.*

At Tripoli none of this applied. On the contrary, the great proportion of a battleship's complement, several hundred highly skilled and specialized officers and men, were to be sent to the bottom with their ship. The nature of the operation precluded the application of the voluntary principle. If a whole host of Engine Room Artificers, Stokers, Cooks and others whose action stations kept them well below decks, were to come ashore in Alexandria before the *Barham* sailed, any chance of maintaining security as to the objective would be hopelessly compromised. And how, in the absence of a great part of her people, was the ship to be fought and sailed through the dangerous waters that she must traverse? Clearly if the operation were to be undertaken not only the *Barham* herself but most of her company would sail from Alexandria under a sentence of death to which the Commander-in-Chief had given his consent. Not only was this a moral outrage: it would also deprive him of the authority to call on his officers and men to face the bloody campaigns that they knew as well as he were to come close to the limits of what flesh and blood could bear. He would, in a word, be denied the one resource in which he knew himself to abound – leadership.

How far and by what means did this quality communicate itself to the officers and men of the Mediterranean Fleet? There are many

---

*This is the generally received version of the remark. But Sir Michael Culme-Seymour's recollection is of hearing one of his fellow staff officers who had accompanied Cunningham to a Commander-in-Chiefs' meeting in Cairo repeating it on his return as: 'It takes two years to build a battleship: it would take two hundred to rebuild the Commonwealth'. Many of the soldiers to be rescued were Australians or New Zealanders and Cunningham remembered the damage done at Gallipoli a generation earlier.

answers, some of them contradictory and none definitive. Yet almost all throw some light on his character. About the most obvious ingredients of leadership there is no difficulty. Moral and physical courage he possessed in an exceptional degree. Decisiveness in action, professional knowledge and judgement, loyalty and generosity to subordinates and the power to inspire these qualities in reciprocity, stamina both physical and intellectual, he had all these. Rarest of all he had the self-restraint not to interfere with the conduct of operations which he had entrusted to a subordinate. One wonders how Admiral Vian would have got on at the Second Battle of Sirte, that classic of successful defence of a convoy against superior forces, if Pound and Churchill had been in Naval Headquarters at Alexandria instead of Cunningham, watching every move, receiving every signal and originating none. It was the last great victory of his long command, a year after the events with which we are now concerned, but perhaps the most striking instance of this virtue.

So far so unexceptionable. But all these qualities were evident only to those who were in direct touch with him, either because they were on his staff, or sailing with him aboard the *Warspite*, or, as flag officers or senior captains commanding cruisers or divisions of destroyers, in regular personal contact. Cunningham's horror of any form of publicity, above all of personal publicity, militated against what might be termed the projection of his image. In this respect he and Field Marshal Montgomery stand at opposite ends of the spectrum amongst the great captains of the Second War.

Friends of my own generation who were serving as junior officers in the Mediterranean Fleet but had no direct contact with him certainly seem to have derived little inspiration from the Commander-in-Chief. My brother who served in *Formidable* exchanging into a corvette when she was damaged so severely that she had to leave the station made little mention of him in his letters and that little unenthusiastic. Certainly he found his successors even less impressive. And this reaction, the usual one among fighting men towards their more distant superiors, seems to have been common.

Unless a commander takes pains to counteract it it is all but inevitable. The Tobruk convoys with which my brother saw much service cost much and achieved little. Those who saw these effects at first hand no doubt attributed them to inept direction. Cunningham himself clearly came to regret his undertaking to supply Tobruk. He had given it in a spirit of generosity towards comrades in arms whom he saw to be hard pressed. He was all the more bitter towards the lack of recognition shown to the navy in Churchill's references to the gallantry with which the soldiers had held on to this battered, beleaguered outpost. But none of this was, or could have been, made known at the time.

With some ships, particularly those which had been on the station from the summer of 1940, there were real anxieties that officers and men were reaching breaking-point. Cunningham himself never lost an opportunity of leading the fleet to sea. He and his staff worked close to *Warspite*'s berth in Alexandria and could be on board in half an hour. He steadfastly resisted the pressure from his army and air force colleagues and from the government in London to move his headquarters to Cairo to facilitate inter-service consultation. He had been appointed to command the battle fleet and he did not intend to delegate this responsibility. But to take the battle fleet to sea without air cover against the most formidable air force in the world was to court irretrievable disaster. Even with a solitary and all too vulnerable carrier it was risky enough. The cruisers and destroyers that had to bear the brunt of the German assault on Greece and Crete could not take him with them if any control of the situation was to be maintained.

A detailed narrative of those heart-breaking months of April and May would serve no purpose beyond that of repetition, itself the hardest trial of a Commander-in-Chief's nerve. Cunningham's own account in his autobiography is especially vivid; Stephen Roskill's in *The War at Sea* masterly, and concise. The losses inflicted were, in his words, '. . . very severe. Two battleships and the aircraft carrier had been damaged, three cruisers and six destroyers sunk and six cruisers and seven destroyers damaged.' A sizeable fleet in

itself. And what was to be set on the credit side of the naval ledger?
Here Roskill's answer rises to the occasion:

> Buried among the mass of official documents accumulated [by
> these operations] – the 'Reports of Proceedings' of the ships
> involved, tables of convoy sailings, copies of signals sent and
> received and statistics of many kinds – some more intimate and
> human papers are, rather surprisingly, to be found. It appears
> that some of the soldiers rescued, NCOs and privates as well as
> officers, wrote down their personal experiences just after their
> escape and left them in the ships which took them off. Thence
> they ultimately reached the Admiralty and so came to be
> incorporated in the official records. In every one of these accounts
> appears the sustaining, almost blind, faith that, if they could only
> reach the sea coast somewhere, the Navy would rescue them. One
> young New Zealander calls it 'the ever-present hope of
> contacting the Navy' and another wrote that during all the long
> retreat in Greece 'our one thought and hope was the Navy'. What
> happened when they reached the sea is vividly recorded by a
> third. 'With a torch we flashed an S.O.S. and, to our tremendous
> relief, we received an answer. It was the Navy on the job – the
> Navy for which we had been hoping and praying all along the
> route' . . . Admiral Cunningham well knew what was required
> when he gave his call to the fleet that 'we must not let them (the
> Army) down.'

He knew, too, the strain and exhaustion of the men on whom he
was calling. Earlier in the year he had noticed, with sympathy and
without censure, two young seamen in the *Warspite* 'literally pea-
green' after a dive-bombing attack. Subjected to such an ordeal day
after day, sometimes hour after hour, without any sign of
protection or hope of easement and above all without rest or
recuperation ashore or in harbour, it was not only the young and the
untried who showed signs of breaking. In the usual measured terms
of a letter to the First Sea Lord Cunningham wrote on 3 May: 'I have

been a little concerned . . . in signs of strain appearing among officers and ratings. Particularly in the anti-aircraft cruisers but it has also appeared in the destroyers. The former have had a gruelling time since [the reinforcement and subsequent evacuation of Greece] started; never a sea trip without being bombed. The Captain of [one] has gone under and we have had to relieve some officers and ratings in [another] . . . We'll hold on somehow I'm sure but this air superiority is the devil.'

Again on the 18th he wrote 'I am a little unhappy about *Gloucester*'s ship's company. They have been a long time from home and have taken more bombs and mines than any other ship out here.' She was lost ten days later off Crete.

Mutiny is a taboo subject in official histories. Did Cunningham mean that he saw premonitory signs in these ships so unremittingly and, as far as their companies could see, unrewardingly exposed to attack against which they had no effective defence? It would be no insult to the memory of brave men to contemplate the possibility. It would not have been, in their eyes, refusal of duty in the face of the enemy so much as a protest against what seemed a reckless, useless squandering of courage and of life freely offered. They were not to know that their Commander-in-Chief was pressing in season and out for immediate air reinforcement on a scale beyond anything that the government was ready to contemplate. What they did see was a style of leadership that insisted on minute details of discipline, for instance in matters of dress, and that made no public admission of the ordeals undergone. 'I see you've been peppered a bit,' Cunningham is said to have remarked on going aboard a cruiser that had returned badly mauled to Alexandria. The sailors drawn up on the quarterdeck broke ranks and were narrowly prevented from throwing him into the harbour. Such is the story that was common fame in Alexandria when a friend of mine arrived there in the early summer of 1941.

Whether or not this particular incident took place there is plenty of evidence that Cunningham's style of leadership worked best at point-blank. It had, after all, been formed in the small interpenetrative milieu of a destroyer. Here as a lifelong succession of letters from ratings who had served with him testify it could attract a strong personal loyalty as it did in the intimate world of those who served on his staff or held commands immediately under him. And even here as one of his most devoted admirers Admiral Oliver pointed out in a passage already quoted some formidable outworks and barriers had first to be negotiated. It was the style of a man who did not mean to make any concessions.

Least of all would he make them to himself. Well aware that he was by no means the Prime Minister's favourite commander he had not hesitated to show his anger when orders were issued from London that conflicted with his own operational direction of the Battle of Crete. When it was over he sent a long signal to the First Sea Lord which he knew the Prime Minister would see:

There is no hiding the fact that in our battle with the German Air Force we have been badly battered. No anti-aircraft fire will deal with the simultaneous attacks of ten or twenty aircraft.

Our losses are very heavy. *Warspite*, *Barham* and *Formidable* out of action for some months. *Orion* and *Dido* in a terrible mess and I have just heard that *Perth* has been hit to-day. Eight destroyers lost outright and several badly damaged. All this not counting *Gloucester* and *Fiji*. I fear the casualties are well over 2,000 dead.

I would not mind if we had inflicted corresponding damage on the enemy but I fear we have achieved little beyond preventing a sea-borne landing in Crete . . . I suppose we shall learn our lesson in time that the navy and army cannot make up for the lack of air forces . . .

And now about my personal position. I hear that the P.M. has removed Longmore (replacing a first-class man with a second-class in my opinion). It may be that he or the Admiralty would like a change in command of the fleet out here. If this is so, I shall not feel in any way annoyed, more especially as it may be that the happenings of the last few days may have shaken the faith of the personnel of the fleet in my handling of affairs.

Whatever Churchill might feel – and it is hard not to suspect a readiness to doubt Cunningham's fighting spirit – Pound was entirely confident in him and probably grateful to have such a counterpoise to Prime Ministerial incursions into the conduct of the war at sea. The command was not an enviable one. It was all commitments and precious few resources. Tobruk and Malta were at best a steady drain on an already enfeebled fleet and might at any moment exact a crippling cost. And without Malta there would be nothing to stop the Germans and Italians running in all the troops and supplies that Rommel needed to win the war in the Middle East. To these commitments the Syrian campaign was added within two weeks of the loss of Crete. The French naval and air forces, commanded by a General who had not concealed his pro-German inclinations, were of high quality and cost ships, men and aircraft that could ill be spared. Hardly was that campaign ended before an offensive was launched against the German army in the Western Desert. Its failure sentenced the navy to another spell of punishment on the Tobruk run. Cunningham does not conceal his opinion that the responsibility for this ill-conceived, inadequately supported assault on a formidable opponent was Churchill's. But the forfeit was paid by Wavell, who was immediately relieved of his command. Much as Cunningham had valued Longmore, his air force colleague, he held Wavell in the highest honour and showed it by flying from Alexandria to see him off from Cairo airport at five in the morning before returning to a normal day's work.

For all that summer of 1941, when both sides were building up their armies in North Africa for the trial of strength that must come, there was little that the surface forces of the Mediterranean fleet could do to interrupt the convoys from Italian ports to Tripoli and Benghazi. Only the submarines based on Malta could take the offensive. It was, like the Battle of Britain, a campaign of exhausting, relentless ferocity conducted by a tiny proportion of the forces to which it was crucial, virtually isolated from their companions in arms and virtually impossible to relieve or replace. The battle fleet in Alexandria, without even a carrier let alone land-based air support, without enough destroyers to form a screen against U-boats, could not steam 500 miles to the Central Mediterranean with any hope of arriving in a state to inflict damage on the enemy. The best that it could do was to make feints in the Eastern Mediterranean that might enable a fast convoy to be slipped into Malta. Cunningham's exasperation at the role thus forced on him was not soothed by the Prime Minister's exhortations to do all that he could to stop the flow of petrol and munitions to Libya. He made it plain that the point had not escaped him. That was why, in season and out, he had never ceased to press for air reinforcements for Malta. Once Malta could be brought into play instead of lying on a life-support machine things would be very different.

By the autumn he had proved his contention. Fighters had been flown in from carriers sailing from Gibraltar, and a great part of the German air forces in Sicily had been withdrawn for service in Russia, invaded in June. Thus by late October Cunningham committed a small force of cruisers and destroyers to Malta with such devastating results that the Germans had no alternative to an all-out air offensive against the island.

This was forced on them by the launching in November of a successful British attack. Cyrenaica was rapidly recaptured, providing air bases from which protection and reconnaissance could enhance the successes of the Malta squadron. If action were not taken Rommel's armour would be immobilized for lack of fuel. Early in December the Luftwaffe was back in even greater numbers than before. For the next few months Malta was to feel its full fury. Within days the surface forces had been overwhelmed. Their battered remnants were withdrawn from the Grand Harbour and once again the life of the island on which everything rested hung by a thread. This was the reality with which the Commander-in-Chief had to contend. How little it had been apprehended by the Prime Minister can be gauged by the fact that it was only at the end of October that the Chiefs of Staff had nerved themselves to postpone consideration of his plan – Operation 'Whipcord' – for the immediate invasion of Sicily, a project to which Cunningham had recorded his decided opposition until the whole of Libya and Tripolitania were in our hands.

Towards the end of November Cunningham took the Battle Fleet to sea, flying his flag in the *Queen Elizabeth*. The object was to cover the light forces still operating from Malta against a possible sortie of Italian battleships in support of two large convoys bound for Benghazi. The result was the loss of the battleship *Barham* in one of the most daring and successful U-boat attacks of the whole war. It was the first time in this war that a British battleship had been sunk at sea.* This blow, heavy in loss of life, was followed by a bloodless *coup de grâce*. On 19 December the *Valiant* and the *Queen Elizabeth* were severely damaged at their moorings in Alexandria harbour by a brilliantly executed human torpedo attack carried out by half a dozen Italian submariners. This disaster may fairly be imputed to Cunningham's obstinacy in retaining an admiral in charge of harbour defence who was not up to the job. His staff had repeatedly warned him of this; but the admiral had been in his term at Dartmouth and that was an end of the matter.

Swift action was taken to disguise the extent of the incapacitation from the reconnaissance aircraft that would be overhead in the morning. But in effect the Mediterranean fleet was now without a battle squadron. Its hope of regaining one or even of retaining its cruiser strength in the face of the calamitous defeats that were following each other in the Far East could be abandoned. The longed for opportunity of fleet operations in the Central Mediterranean now that Cyrenaica was ours had evaporated before it could be grasped. Indeed the total denial of naval initiative robbed the army of the fruits of victory. Enemy convoys sped across the narrows unmolested, except for the heroic efforts of submarines which could hardly enter or leave Malta without serious risk of mines and which had to lie submerged during daylight hours in

*The *Hood*, sunk by the *Bismarck*, was a battlecruiser.

harbour. The Germans grew rapidly stronger. On 21 January they launched a successful counter-offensive and Benghazi which had just with infinite labour been equipped to receive the main supplies of the Eighth Army had precipitately to be abandoned. The rest of Cyrenaica soon followed. Everything was to do again and the situation of Malta was more perilous than ever.

At this blackest of moments Cunningham received one substantial reinforcement. Philip Vian, whom he had picked out as a young officer in destroyers and whom on his promotion to captain he had specially requested to command a flotilla when war seemed to threaten over Italy's invasion of Abyssinia, had vindicated his judgement by a series of brilliant and daring actions. On 1 November Vian hoisted his flag in command of the 15th Cruiser Squadron in Alexandria. The three light cruisers of which it consisted had become within two months the main force, the sole force, at Cunningham's disposal to pit against the battleships and heavy cruisers of the Italian fleet.

The need to risk so desperate a throw soon presented itself. Malta, the one position that must not be lost, made sure of that. In mid-February Vian took his ships to sea to cover a convoy of three fast merchantmen and to bring out three empty ones together with a fleet oiler which had discharged her cargo. All the loaded merchantmen were bombed on passage and had to be sunk. Three weeks later Vian's flagship was sunk by a U-boat as he was escorting the newly joined cruiser *Cleopatra* from Malta to Alexandria. Transferring his flag to the new arrival he sailed in her on yet another attempt to run a convoy in before it was too late.

No more brilliant, no more gallant action was fought during the whole war at sea than this classic defence of a convoy against superior forces. Known to history as the Second Battle of Sirte it has been well described in the official history and a number of memoirs including Cunningham's. Captain Pack in his life of Cunningham prints a letter from Admiral Sir Guy Grantham, Vian's flag captain in the *Cleopatra*, which in the most calm and measured way enables the reader to see just how frightening it must have been. The Italian gunnery – there were two eight-inch cruisers and one six-inch as well as a battleship – was very good.

> Being close straddled by 15-inch shells was quite a noisy experience; they made a tremendous bang when they hit the water. At the same time we were being bombed and we could see the convoy being attacked by many waves of bombers. We used our three forward turrets for firing at the enemy ships, and the two after turrets against aircraft.
>
> We, in *Cleopatra*, were hit only once, by a 6-inch shell which I saw coming apparently straight at me, though it sheered off at the last moment and hit the starboard fore-corner of the bridge, where Philip normally stood or sat on his stool chair . . . he was luckily having a quick look at our position in the chart house. That shell killed 14 and brought down all our W/T aerials.

The tactics of the battle, discussed between Cunningham and Vian, and expounded at a conference of captains, depended on the laying of a smokescreen behind which the convoy could retire while the cruisers and destroyers of the protecting force nipped in and out to fire their guns and discharge their torpedoes. Fortune in this case favoured the brave. A strong wind blew the smoke towards the attackers and a rising sea lessened the enemy's advantage of superior speed. The professionalism of the planning, the brilliant ship-handling in manoeuvres that had been carefully rehearsed, above all the complete understanding of the Admiral's purpose and method by his captains surely justify the epithet Nelsonic.

The battle was fought on 22 March. On the 24th two of the merchantmen entered the Grand Harbour and a third ship carrying oil fuel, hit and disabled only eight miles out, was towed to a small harbour on the south side of the island. Subsequent air attack denied Malta the full measure of even this dear-bought relief; but to have brought in anything against such odds was a triumph. A week later, in the greatest secrecy, Cunningham hauled down his flag as Commander-in-Chief Mediterranean.

The ending of this great command thus contained the elements that had characterized it from the beginning. A victory had been won, in the highest traditions of the Royal Navy, by skill and courage, teamwork and leadership, against a much stronger enemy. Malta, constantly battered and now beset from every side, had been narrowly and slenderly relieved. The Commander-in-Chief, yearning with every fibre to be leading his battle squadron into action had been condemned by the ceaseless overstretching of seriously diminished forces to follow the course of this naval Agincourt in his office in Alexandria. We are fortunate in having an eyewitness account of this, given to Captain Pack by the army liaison officer, who perhaps noticed things that a naval officer would have taken for granted. He saw at once how moved Cunningham was by the dangers to which his men were exposed and which he could not share. He saw him envisaging the whole course of the action, anticipating Vian's moves and shouting with delight when he made them. He admired the rigid self-control with which the Commander-in-Chief practised what he preached about non-interference with a subordinate to whom he had entrusted control of an operation, even when this operation was one on which he had been forced to stake not only the survival of Malta but the existence of his fleet. Only when action had been broken off and the Italians were retiring at full speed did he issue an order, that an anti-aircraft cruiser should be detached from the fleet to support the convoy on its onward voyage to Malta.

When Vian's ships entered harbour at noon on the 24th Cunningham signalled 'Well done 15th Cruiser Squadron and destroyers'. For one who carried the cult of the Silent Service to the edge of paranoia it was a Pindaric ode. Even more remarkably after hesitating at so uninhibited a gesture of approbation he joined in cheering them in.

* * *

Cunningham did not want to give up the Mediterranean command. A month or two earlier he had considered the question as dispassionately as he could in a letter to the First Sea Lord. He had, he pointed out, held the post for just short of three years so that it would be in the order of things for him to be relieved. But he felt fit and ready to carry on. In particular he did not wish to leave at a moment when the fortunes of the fleet were at their lowest and the dangers higher than ever. When there were so few ships the main responsibility of the Commander-in-Chief must lie, as his had lain for the past months, very much in the politico-strategic field. In such a situation experience, personal prestige and a record of achievement must carry weight. From his own point of view the command was still the most important one available. There might not for the moment be many ships: but there were 25,000 officers and men.

There were also, much to his initial annoyance, some 40 Wrens. His staff had recognized that a number of jobs would be better done by women and that the manpower saved would increase the numbers available for reliefs and replacements in the fleet. Foreseeing his likely reaction they had quietly arranged with the Admiralty to put this into effect. The first detachment sailed from England in the early autumn of 1941 on the long passage round the Cape of Good Hope. Not till they had reached Massawa in the Red Sea did Cunningham realize what had been done in his name. He exploded and insisted that they should be immediately rerouted to Singapore. While they were still on passage the Japanese declaration of war, followed almost at once by the loss of the *Prince of Wales* and the *Repulse*, caused the vessel to be recalled. Thus by the time the Wrens actually arrived they had been for several months in enforced idleness in an overwhelmingly masculine society and several of them were pregnant. 'What did I tell you?' thundered the Commander-in-Chief. But even in the short time before he hauled down his flag he admitted the value of their services and asked for reinforcements.

Pound did not answer Cunningham's letter at once. But in the middle of March he told him that he wished him to succeed Admiral Sir Charles Little as his personal representative at the head of the Admiralty Delegation in Washington. He would be relieved, in the strictest secrecy, by his second-in-command on 1 April until his designated successor Sir Henry Harwood could be sent out from London. Cunningham's reply was markedly unenthusiastic. He had no aptitude for the Washington job and Sir Charles Little would do it far better. Harwood had, in his opinion, neither the seniority nor the experience of command nor the personal reputation in the service to undertake such responsibilities or to justify so exceptional a promotion – he was only a very junior Rear-Admiral and had not served in that rank at sea. He himself, he repeated, would be more than ready to carry on. No notice was taken of his objections or of his offer. He was to return to London to discuss his future appointment with the First Sea Lord and the Prime Minister.

Cunningham's reservations as to the qualifications of his successor were to be too soon and too expensively justified. But Pound and Churchill certainly had reasons for thinking a change at the top desirable. Relations between the service chiefs in the Middle East were not what they had been in the days of Longmore and Wavell. Cunningham and Tedder were not on good terms, and Wavell's successor, Auchinleck, had, it appears, given Cunningham the impression that he regarded himself as bearing with him some aura of vice-regal authority from his long service in India. Matters had been made worse by the summary dismissal of Cunningham's brother, Alan, the victor of the East African campaign, from the command of the Eighth Army on the very eve of the offensive launched in November 1941. Cunningham in his private letters at the time attributed this to Churchill in the bitterest terms: 'He has in my opinion been most disgracefully and unjustly treated. Poor Alan he went into the battle with such high hopes and things would have gone just as well and probably better had he been left in command. It's a most disgraceful business and the worst of it is that in war time there is no redress.' (16 December 1941.)

'I was quite furious when I read Churchill's speech about Alan's relief. He was made the scapegoat for Churchill's boasting before the battle opened.' (30 December 1941.)

Auchinleck's responsibility is not mentioned. Yet there is not the slightest doubt that it was his decision, and not Churchill's, to remove General Cunningham from his command and that he had every reason to do so. By the evidence of the men on the spot and by agreement of later historians Alan Cunningham was exhausted and in no condition to direct a major campaign. What is more A. B. Cunningham had received a long and courteous letter written on 26 November in his own hand by his fellow Commander-in-Chief immediately after a personal visit to Eighth Army Headquarters: 'I find that the tremendous strain of the past week has been too much for him.' The admiral commanding the Mediterranean fleet knew all about such things and that there was no disgrace in them though there must be disappointment. He himself, to take but one instance, had sent Algernon Willis, his Chief of Staff, home, with the highest possible encomium on his service, because he had worn himself out. The tone of his letters makes it clear that he did not accept the diagnosis. In which case cordiality between the two commanders can hardly have been expected. That this was widely felt by officers under their command is remarked on as common knowledge in a letter written by my brother after Cunningham's relief was made public.

The fact that Cunningham preferred in private to blame the Prime Minister for what he considered the injustice done to his brother is not surprising. As has been pointed out all his instincts and prejudices, strong forces in so strong a character, led him to look on Churchill as a bounder and an adventurer. He much preferred the restraint and dignity of politicians such as Lord Halifax. But he was far too serious and capable an officer to have allowed himself to be influenced by prejudice, however strong, against the man responsible for the whole conduct of the war if Churchill had treated him with the courtesy and loyalty that men joined in authority have a right to expect from one another. This is exactly what he had failed to do. From the start he had let it be seen that he thought Cunningham – Cunningham! – hesitant, even timid. When almost at once Cunningham had shown the rarest courage over the disarming of the French ships in Alexandria, Churchill had been by turns bullying, petulant and ungenerous. Towards Cunningham's colleagues in those unhappy affairs at the other end of the Mediterranean he had shown himself vindictive and unfair. Over Greece and Crete he had once again shown himself distrustful of Cunningham's offensive spirit – and this after the victories of Taranto and Matapan. One could go on; Cunningham's recollection could certainly have gone on. And no doubt such recollections strengthened his prejudices instead of curbing them. Cunningham was not a vain man and had a horror of anything that smacked of boastfulness. But he had a proper sense of his achievements, or, as he would have put it, the achievements of the officers and men he had had the honour to command. He felt no false humility towards the great war leader he was on his way to meet.

What did Churchill think about him? In the sunset glow of war memoirs as in lapidary inscriptions a man is not upon oath. Besides when he came to write them he and Cunningham had come to know each other as intimate colleagues in the closing stages of the war. If we turn to Mr Martin Gilbert's monumental biography we will not find much to enlighten us. The personal relations between the Prime Minister and his Commander-in-Chief occupy a small part of that vast canvas compared with those between the great man and his shorthand typists. Almost the only personal information about Cunningham is the author's gratuitous but misleading statement that he was the cousin of Sir John Cunningham, the Admiral who succeeded to the Mediterranean command in the last years of the war. They were in fact no relation to each other.

Firsthand contemporary evidence of Churchill's opinion is to be found in a remarkably candid and refreshing letter from Admiral Sir John Tovey, who had been recalled in the autumn of 1940 from his appointment as Cunningham's second-in-command to be offered the Home Fleet. The letter, dated 19 October 1940 and marked personal to Cunningham, describes an intimate dinner with Churchill.

You know the P.M. much better than I do and you will

understand how I loved him at first sight, but he made some such astounding statements about naval warfare both at home and abroad, I still don't know whether he was wanting to find out if I was prepared to applaud everything he said or whether he really believes half what he says . . .

I found myself being extremely argumentative. The P.M. was quite charming and, I believe, really enjoyed every minute of it and all he said was that he didn't mind my being absolutely outspoken, in fact that he liked it but that one must keep one's mind open to honest conviction – a very fair remark. I only hope he succeeded . . .

He actually stated that he considered you were too pussy-foot in your dealings with Godfroy at the time of Oran . . .

The expression 'pussy-foot' had got me rather on the raw and I found I had a good deal more to tell him of you and your doings, eventually he wanted to send off a signal there and then to you saying that after a long talk with me he had the profoundest confidence in you and appreciated that you were taking every offensive action possible . . .

That evening was a great success, though I am a little afraid the P.M.'s opinion of me was considerably enhanced by my appreciation of his brandy . . .

Cunningham's departure from Alexandria had been furtive so as not to give comfort to the King's enemies. He had been much moved to find the station platform crowded with naval officers. It had been a grief not to be allowed to say goodbye and to express the deep gratitude and admiration he felt for companions-in-arms who had done the best things in the worst of times. He was perhaps not less moved if by rather different feelings at finding the Board of Admiralty waiting on the platform at Paddington to honour his return to England. The Prime Minister himself attended the luncheon to which their Lordships then entertained him.

Nothing could have been more handsome. Yet Cunningham reserved a certain dour scepticism. It was hardly promotion for the successful holder of the most important of wartime commands to go to Washington as a kind of glorified naval attaché. In fact to his deep indignation the terms on which the appointment was offered were even below that. On 11 June, some five or six weeks after his arrival in London he wrote to his aunt:

> They will not give me proper status in Washington and are trying to pay me less than our Naval Attaché over there. So I have refused to go and have written a letter requesting permission to withdraw my acceptance of the appointment. Although I have shown it to the First Lord I have not actually sent it in, giving him time to see what he can do. Of course it is W. C. who is the nigger in the woodpile and he has undoubtedly some ulterior motive.
>
> I lunched with him and Mrs Churchill at 10 Downing St on Tuesday. I liked her very much. I tried to bring him to the point but he slid out of it every time, though I made it quite clear to him that the question of my going to the USA was not yet settled. He has now asked me to dine and sleep at Chequers on Sunday and I am going. I know he has some proposition to put to me which at lunch he didn't think I was in the mood to accept. He's in for the surprise of his life when he makes it as I know what it is – nothing to do with going to the USA.

The half-amused tone of this passage does not attempt to disguise the resentment, partly personal but mostly professional, which its writer felt. He had been given a hero's welcome but, in the tactful formula used by the bankers when they return a cheque to its drawer, the words and figures did not agree. What was Churchill's game? What did Cunningham himself think that his next appointment ought to be?

The first question is easily answered. Churchill wanted Cunningham to replace Tovey as Commander-in-Chief Home Fleet. The offer was made during the visit to Chequers, recalled by Cunningham in a letter to Stephen Roskill written in September 1961. The relevant passage, printed in Roskill's *Churchill and the*

Admirals (p. 142) reads as follows:

> WSC: 'Of course there is no reason why you should go to Washington.' [Cunningham had made no secret of his sense of insult.]
> ABC: 'I thought that was the reason for my being brought home.'
> WSC: 'No, I want you to go to the Home Fleet.'
> ABC: 'But you have a very good Admiral there already, Sir John Tovey.'
> WSC: 'Oh, I want you to relieve Admiral Tovey.'
> ABC (rather angry): 'If Tovey drops dead on his bridge I will certainly relieve him. Otherwise not.'

Cunningham was angry because he saw the Prime Minister treating his old friend and fellow Commander-in-Chief in exactly the way that had outraged him in the Mediterranean. Churchill wanted to get rid of Tovey because he had warned with the outspokenness originally enjoined on him that the continuation of the convoys to North Russia during the perpetual daylight of the Arctic summer would risk a major disaster. Rather than accept the good faith and professional competence of the man on the spot Churchill once again preferred to impute lack of fighting spirit. He certainly found plenty of it in Cunningham who had clearly been informed by Pound, the First Sea Lord, as to what was in the wind. Hence his confidence in his foreknowledge of Churchill's intentions, expressed in his letter to his aunt. Hence too his showing his unsent letter of refusal of the Washington appointment to Alexander, the First Lord, who, he knew, would at once communicate its contents to the Prime Minister. He was determined that Churchill should understand that he wasn't going to put up with any nonsense. This at least was made clear in the course of the evening at Chequers. 'We had a heart to heart talk for about one and a half hours,' he wrote to his aunt on 16 June. 'We found many points both of agreement and disagreement and I found him quite ready to listen. We went to bed at 2.30 a.m. . . . . I think it is likely we shall get away [to Washington] this week. But I don't go until the Treasury make the right arrangements.' Churchill was himself about to pay a visit to Roosevelt. 'The Prime Minister had asked me to travel with him by sea; but I had refused. His invitation did not include my wife, and I did not think she would care to fly the Atlantic without me.' This statement in *A Sailor's Odyssey* reinforces the tone of stiffness, of the need to assert a status that was being slighted. It is the odder because the Prime Minister did not in fact go by sea but much enjoyed the experience of being allowed to control the movements of a large aircraft.

What did Cunningham hope for when he returned to England on hauling down his flag as Commander-in-Chief Mediterranean? Admiral Dick who worked as closely with him and knew him as well as any thinks that he expected to succeed Pound as First Sea Lord and was much hurt that no such offer was made. The first three years of the war at sea had been enough to wear out a younger and fitter man. Pound, not surprisingly, was already showing signs of strain. This was intensified by the grave illness of his wife on whose support this solitary, unclubbable man largely depended. How ill she was was evidenced by his absence from the platform at Paddington when the Board turned out to welcome Cunningham home. She died in July of the following year. Pound resigned two months later and himself died in October. He had fought a good fight. But it may be that he should not have been left so long without relief.

Indeed at their first private interview Pound had told Cunningham that he was much upset by reports that Churchill was dissatisfied with his performance and wished to replace him by Mountbatten. What did Cunningham think he ought to do? It was, as Stephen Roskill pointed out in *Churchill and the Admirals* an embarrassing question since, if Pound were to resign, his obvious successor was the man he was talking to. Cunningham, who had, as a connoisseur of destroyer captains, no great opinion of Mountbatten's record in inflicting damage on the enemy, insisted that Pound should on no account be accessory to such a disaster. He must 'glue himself to his chair'. Philip Ziegler in his biography of Mountbatten points out that Ismay, Churchill's liaison officer with the Chiefs of Staff, is unequivocally on record that Churchill had no such intention. It would have been preposterous to have appointed an officer whose substantive rank was only that of a captain above the whole body of admirals on the active list, some of whom had discharged the highest commands with conspicuous success and even, in the case of Vian and of Cunningham himself, had already taken their place among the great sea officers of our history. Even Churchill with his passion for putting the cat among the naval pigeons must have known perfectly well that he could not effect such a substitution. Furthermore there is a good deal of evidence that he was genuinely fond of Pound and rightly judged that among the senior naval officers who were, so to speak, *papabile*, Pound would be the most accommodating, the least likely to dig in his heels over the intrusion of a civilian head of government into the conduct of operations. What then was the point of upsetting him? Was it, perhaps, simply to shake his nerve in daring to oppose Churchill's desire to replace Tovey in the Home Fleet?

During his time in England, perhaps as a result of his conversations with Churchill, Cunningham drafted a memorandum on the question of Command in the Middle East. He had consistently opposed the idea of a unified Supreme Command and continued to do so. But, he argued, if there *were* to be a Supreme Commander in that theatre it should be a naval officer: 'This is written in no narrow spirit of service rivalry but I feel that the tendency to place large areas of the globe in military control needs giving pause in areas where the primary factor is control of the sea. We should consider it strange were a German Admiral to control the armies on the Russian front. This is a war of seapower, our greatness has been built up on our aptitude for sea warfare and we should be chary of turning the use of this weapon over to those who have not been trained primarily to that end.' Churchill's view of the naval profession on the other hand was essentially seventeenth-century, when Generals at Sea, who had gained their experience in land fighting, were appointed to direct the motions of the masters of vessels who were not to concern themselves with matters that were too high for them. In May 1943 when Brooke as head of the Chiefs of Staff was urging Cunningham's name as the best man for the proposed South East Asia Supreme Command, Churchill wrote: 'I do not think that a sailor is well-qualified for a command of this character. The sea-faring and scientific technique of the naval profession makes such severe demands upon the training of naval men, that they have very rarely the time or opportunity to study military history and the art of war in general.' Here, alive and kicking, is the distinction between the tarpaulins and the gentlemen that Pepys had set out to abolish two-and-a-half centuries earlier.

* * *

Cunningham and his wife flew to Washington at the end of June. He had obtained satisfaction, if not gratification, on the question of pay and status. He had been honoured by a baronetcy, which he set no store by and only accepted as a token of recognition and respect to the achievements of the navy in the Mediterranean. He and Churchill had had the first opportunity to size each other up. It had not been all wine and roses but things might easily have gone much worse.

The Washington appointment was congenial in its essence but difficult and trying in its incidentals. Cunningham was, for so apparently insular a man, notably good at getting on with foreigners and had in any case many friends in the US navy from his previous service on the station. On the other hand he disliked serving ashore, especially in wartime. He hated towns, and Washington in the summer is not the most agreeable of climates. He was both physically and temperamentally ill-suited to the social life of eating and drinking that such a post required. He had had two operations for stomach ulcers between the wars and was to be intermittently troubled by his digestion for the rest of his career.

The object of Cunningham's mission was the establishment of

trust and co-operation between the American and English service chiefs who were to be charged with common action on a gigantic scale. Where this action was to take place was hardly settled by the time of Cunningham's arrival. Roosevelt had wanted a direct assault on Europe. Churchill argued, in the event successfully, for a North African invasion which would secure the Mediterranean while the enormous forces and supplies required for a campaign against the Germans in Western Europe were being built up. Once the objective had been chosen there still remained the question of command. How was it to be divided between the two countries, between the two American and three British services, and yet be suffused with the unity that experience showed to be the first condition of success?

A good start had been made before Cunningham appeared on the scene. Churchill's service to his country was never more valuable than in his assiduous cultivation of the closest relations with the President. For the soldiers Dill on the British side, Marshall and Bedell Smith on the American had won everyone's confidence and respect. Admiral Sir Charles Little, Cunningham's predecessor, had by all accounts done very well. But in Fleet Admiral Ernest J. King, USN he was up against a fire-eater. A strong authoritarian personality, he dominated his service as Jacky Fisher had done his but unlike Fisher was devoid of charm, wit, courtesy or even common politeness. His military colleagues he treated as of little account; but for the Royal Navy he nourished a scornful hostility. Cunningham could be patient when he had to be but soon found no reason to persist in so unnatural a posture. The fur flew. King never reached an easy working relationship with his British colleague but he recognized that now and then he might have to give way to him. With all the other American service chiefs A.B.C. established excellent relationships which prolonged association was only to deepen. There is perhaps no more telling evidence of this than the letter Dill wrote him almost a year later after lunching tête-à-tête with General Marshall. 'I do not tell you this [Marshall's tribute to Cunningham] for your personal gratification! but that you may know how completely the Americans (including King!) trust your judgment and will accept your considered opinion.'

Cunningham was only in Washington for just over three months. During that time some momentous decisions were taken in which he had no small hand. The North African option was confirmed and a date set for landings in the autumn. An American lieutenant-general, recently promoted from colonel, was appointed to the Supreme Command. And the structure of the naval command that would support him was agreed in the form recommended by Cunningham, namely that there should be a single naval Com-mander-in-Chief directly under the Supreme Commander and working alongside him in the closest consultation. The American army chiefs sounded out Cunningham as to his willingness to accept this appointment. He replied guardedly that he had not heard any such proposition from the First Sea Lord but that if he approved he would be proud to serve under an American Supreme Commander.

Thus he embarked on what one of his closest associates from Mediterranean days, Admiral Royer Dick, considers the greatest service he rendered to his country. That was certainly not Dick's view at the time. He had accompanied him to Washington as he was to accompany him to North Africa. When Cunningham told him of his proposed appointment as naval Commander-in-Chief to serve under Eisenhower, Dick reproved him in outspoken terms. It was absurd and unfitting that a senior admiral who had won the most notable victories of the war should consent to play second fiddle to an unknown American soldier with no experience of war, who had never commanded a formation larger than a company and who had till this sudden factitious promotion only reached the rank of colonel. Cunningham's reply, as recalled by Admiral Dick in his description of this scene, was 'If I haven't got him in my pocket after six weeks I'll go.'

In fact he rose far above that limited, self-defensive ambition. He gave Eisenhower the support and the loyalty that enabled him to develop his self-confidence while learning the ropes and thus to grow to the full height of a personality whose courage and generosity won reconciliation and respect from the formidable collection of warriors and statesmen who had, somehow, to be held together. It is Cunningham's supreme contribution to the making of Eisenhower that Admiral Dick came to see as the most valuable of all his achievements.

That Eisenhower with the humility of greatness recognized his debt to Cunningham is refreshingly attested by his own letters to him. Writing on 10 May 1945 in the glow of final victory he remembered the days of anxiety and self-doubt when he and Cunningham had been waiting at Gibraltar for the assault convoys to come through in November 1942:

> Just the other day someone asked me what particular period I would probably remember longest . . . The subject was intriguing enough to demand an hour's conversation and out of it I came to the conclusion that the hours you and I spent together in the dripping tunnels of Gibraltar will probably remain as long in my memory as will any other. It was there I first understood the indescribable and inescapable strain that comes over one when his part is done – when the issue rests with fate and the fighting men he has committed to action.
>
> Moreover, it was during those hours that I first became well-acquainted with you and really learned that I had a partner in that campaign to whom I could always look with admiration, confidence and affection.

The military and naval conduct of the North African campaign has been well and often described. For his part Cunningham had reassembled the small body of staff officers who had worked with him so well in the Mediterranean. A month of Herculean labour in London had produced the necessary instructions for the largest seaborne invasion yet mounted. In spite of the haste, in spite of the numbers and distances involved, this complicated operation went off without a hitch. One small incident communicated to me by Captain Nigel Pumphrey who was commanding one of the fleet

destroyers escorting the main Algiers convoy shows Cunningham
the commander, warts and all. The convoy had nearly reached
Algiers without incident when a large troopship carrying about
8,000 men was torpedoed. Her Captain gave orders to abandon ship
since although she was only a few miles off Algiers it was clear to
him that she was beyond hope. Cunningham ordered two Hunt
class destroyers to go alongside and take off her troops which they
successfully did. Hunt class destroyers are small vessels and Captain
Pumphrey thought it no mean achievement on their part to have
taken on board so many survivors; in fact he would have thought it a
job for three. But A.B.C., so far from congratulating the two
captains, wished to have them both courtmartialled for not having
taken the troopship in tow and brought her in, in spite of the fact
that she had sunk shortly after being hit. Only the continued
remonstrance of his staff at length dissuaded him.

Cunningham's own knowledge of the sea in which he had spent
the greater part of his naval career was put to fullest use. His
knowledge of, and previous relations with, the French naval
commanders was perhaps even more valuable but might in his view
have been better taken into account. In particular he urged a more
daring strategic plan for the initial assault which would have
included a landing at Bizerta, the great naval base in Tunisia,
instead of limiting the easternmost landings to Algeria. Crucial to
his advice of this policy was the fact that Admiral Esteva was the
naval Commander-in-Chief and deputy governor. The French
troops there were so few that they would not be strong enough to
resist the Germans should they arrive (as they instantly did) and
Cunningham was confident of rallying Esteva to the alliance of
which he had been so fervent an upholder. Esteva in his own letters
to Cunningham written after the war when he was imprisoned,
unfairly as Cunningham thought, confirms this reading of the
situation. Such a stroke would, if successful, have transformed the
campaign. Clearly Cunningham, not a rash strategist or an
armchair dreamer of military might-have-beens, continued to think
it a missed opportunity.

This was at the time the instant reaction of General de Gaulle when to his outraged surprise he was informed of the North African landings. Algiers was less interesting to a man whose chief preoccupation for the past three years had been the control of the Central Mediterranean and the holding of Malta. But in the extraordinary situation brought about by the unlooked for presence of Admiral Darlan, Cunningham's standing had particular value. In the confusion of the first two days when allied authority was by no means clearly established Cunningham sent his Chief of Staff, Commodore Dick, to accompany General Mark Clark and Roosevelt's French candidate for command, General Giraud. Darlan who at first refused to shake hands with any British officer at once made an exception of Dick on hearing that he was Cunningham's representative. Four days later when Eisenhower and Cunningham flew in from Gibraltar Darlan 'greeted me most effusively, shook me warmly by the hand, and said "Thank you for Admiral Godfroy".' The value of what might be termed this 'special relationship' is hard to quantify. But in the six weeks before his assassination Darlan consulted Cunningham, or at least listened to and acted on his recommendations, in his dealings with the still considerable fleet of which he was the titular Admiral. The battleship *Richelieu* at Dakar was preserved to take part in the war. But Godfroy at Alexandria still felt unable to respond to both Darlan's and Cunningham's personal appeals.

The most urgent question was what was going to happen to the large fleet in harbour at Toulon. In the event Admiral de la Borde gave orders for its scuttling. After the war he was tried and condemned to death. His wife and his brother both besought Cunningham to appeal to the French President for a reprieve. Their letters, together with the pencilled draft of Cunningham's simple, dignified letter to Vincent-Auriol are preserved in his papers. The appeal succeeded. He had known and liked de la Borde as he had Esteva, on whose behalf he also wrote privately to the French authorities in the period of vindictiveness and scapegoatery that followed the Liberation. What did he make of Darlan? Three days after their meeting he wrote to his aunt: 'Darlan was most embarrassingly cordial to me but he looked rather a snake and I would not trust him.' Such, to judge from *A Sailor's Odyssey*, remained his opinion although he insists, with characteristic fairness that 'once Darlan made up his mind to throw in his lot with the Allies at the end of 1942, he acted absolutely squarely with us, and was the only man who could have brought North and West Africa in with us. To me personally, he was invariably most cordial, in fact I lunched with him and his wife at the Palais D'Eté the day before his murder.' It is also characteristic of Cunningham not to claim credit for the vindication of his judgement in 1940 that the use of force against the French fleet might prevent a renewal of common action against the Germans. The courage he had shown in Alexandria two and a half years earlier had, though he does not say so, borne fruit.

For a brilliant dissection of the comedies and chicaneries acted out in North Africa at the end of 1942 and the beginning of 1943 the reader should turn to the relevant chapter in François Kersaudy's *Churchill and De Gaulle*. Eisenhower was fortunate in having at his elbow an officer of such integrity and such astuteness as Cunningham. It was a political minefield for a military man, not made safer or easier by the arrival in person of the President of the United States and the Prime Minister of Great Britain; the one the sworn enemy of the Free French movement, the other its professed though resentful champion. On his own naval ground Cunningham had to contend with international as well as operational hazards. Apart from the French, Fleet Admiral Ernest J. King held that American ships should never, if he could help it, come under British command. Since the Moroccan flank of the assault was to be covered and conducted by ships sailing directly across the Atlantic this presented an obstacle to the unity of command. Cunningham negotiated a settlement that gave him control while they were in the zone of the landing. King's mischievous doctrine induced the American Rear-Admiral appointed to take charge at Oran to attempt to bypass Cunningham by dealing directly with Eisenhower. The total failure of this manoeuvre is telling evidence of Cunningham's success in winning the confidence of the Supreme Commander.

The Tunisian campaign had its ups and downs. The Germans, with their backs to the wall for the first time, fought magnificently. But this time the Royal Navy, adequately supported in the air, asserted effective command of the sea in a number of hot actions and at the cost of some losses to enemy submarines. Land communications were so poor that the Allied army had, as in the earlier Eighth Army campaigns, to be supplied by sea; and once again the escorts suffered heavy casualties. Malta, in business once again as a base for offensive operations, enabled British submarines to retaliate in kind. On 21 January Cunningham's masterly conduct of the naval side of the campaign was recognized by his promotion to the rank of Admiral of the Fleet. Both he and his right-hand in the planning of the assault, Admiral Sir Bertram Ramsay, were charged with the preparations for the next stage, the invasion of Sicily, to be undertaken at the earliest possible moment after the ending of the Tunisian campaign.

Malta, the centre of his concern for so much of the recent past, would obviously be the centre of preparations for an attack on Sicily. For this reason towards the end of February Cunningham was, to his profound gratification, once again appointed to the historic post of Commander-in-Chief Mediterranean. Only once before had this great command been held twice by the same man and that was by an admiral of whom no one had ever heard in a period when nothing was going on. His successor at Alexandria, Admiral Harwood, became Commander-in-Chief Levant with responsibility for the Eastern basin and the Red Sea.

On 12 May the last German forces in Tunis surrendered. Four days earlier when it was clear that they had nothing to do but escape Cunningham had issued an order to the destroyers operating off Cape Bon: 'Sink, burn and destroy: let nothing pass.' The German forces still to be encountered in Sicily and Italy were formidable enough without reinforcement from the troops that had given such a good account of themselves under Rommel. And both Cunningham and his brother officers in the destroyers, many of whom had endured the terrible hammering of Greece and Crete, would have been hardly human if they had not wanted to get a bit of their own back. 'You are to sink, burn or destroy.' The words at once call to mind the instructions to admirals in the Dutch wars of Charles II.

From this point the character of the war, or at any rate Cunningham's part of the war, changes. It is enemy territory that is to be bombed, assaulted, occupied; and allied preponderance at sea, already decisive, rapidly becomes overwhelming. At the end of May the apparent reconciliation of hitherto irreconcilable Frenchmen permitted Admiral Godfroy to follow his own inclinations with a clear conscience and rejoin the Allies. Cunningham drew the attention of the Prime Minister, then visiting Algiers, 'to the first verse of the penultimate chapter of Ecclesiastes: "Cast thy bread upon the waters: for thou shalt find it after many days." My innocent remark was rather ill-received.' It was the kind of trumping a trick with a well-known quotation that Mr Churchill particularly enjoyed doing to others. And both he and Cunningham knew that only a few weeks earlier he had tried to encourage Admiral Harwood to threaten Godfroy once more. The scene that gave Cunningham the purest sense of his achievement took place at Malta in mid-June when the cruiser *Aurora* steamed into the Grand Harbour with the King on the bridge acknowledging the cheers of his Maltese subjects crowding the half-ruined palaces and warehouses that lined the shore. That was what he had been fighting for.

The Sicilian campaign followed by the invasion of the mainland and the surrender of the Italian fleet form a climax to Cunningham's long and hard service in the great sea with which his name will be associated until the Royal Navy is itself forgotten. At the opening of the campaign he drew on his knowledge of its weather in judging correctly that the violent wind that threatened the landings would drop by the time for disembarkation. At its end his failure to press the attack on the retreating Germans in their passage of the Straits of Messina was remarked by Stephen Roskill when writing his official history and discussed between them in correspondence. It seems uncharacteristic; and the Admiral had no recollection of any reason for inaction and had evidently never felt any sense of a duty inadequately discharged. He was not given to flattering himself or anyone else so that complacency hardly seems a likely explanation. The Germans were certainly astonished, particularly at the failure of the Allies to use their overwhelming air superiority against an evacuation that took place largely by daylight. The Straits are too narrow – about two-and-a-half miles at the point where most of the troops were crossing – and too heavily defended by well-sited shore batteries to make forays by surface vessels anything but suicidal. But the defences and the ferry-craft were both vulnerable to bombardment from heavy ships standing off. None of the three service chiefs seems to have thought of this. Perhaps the root of the matter may have lain in the indifferent co-operation between them. Montgomery had been characteristically provocative to his colleagues in the signals he had sent requiring a complete change of plan shortly before the invasion. Tedder and Cunningham had never enjoyed the generous comradeship that Cunningham had shared with Wavell and Longmore and which was so fortunately and fully reciprocated in his relations with Eisenhower.

In the Salerno landings early in September Cunningham and his trusted subordinate and old friend Geoffrey Oliver were instrumental in preventing a military disaster. At the height of the German counter-attack which had driven the invaders almost back to their beaches General Mark Clark proposed to exchange part of the forces under his command between one bridgehead and another. Summoned aboard the US admiral's headquarters' ship to expedite this plan Commodore Oliver protested vigorously against a manoeuvre so certain to cause very heavy loss and so likely to result in total defeat and insisted on communicating his views to the naval Commander-in-Chief. Cunningham instantly supported him, promised the hard-pressed Americans immediate naval reinforcement and obtained the concurrence of both the Divisional and the Army Commander of the British forces involved.

Almost at the same moment as the British and American soldiers were fighting their way ashore at Salerno the news was released of the Italian government's withdrawal from the war and the surrender of the fleet. Negotiations had been conducted in the utmost secrecy lest the Germans should get wind of them. In these Cunningham had been represented by Admiral Dick who naturally did not attend the clandestine meetings with his Italian colleagues in full uniform. When the news broke the papers published photographs of the officers signing the initial agreements. Cunningham's fury that his Chief of Staff should have allowed himself to be seen at so historic an occasion in a bush shirt outweighed, so Admiral Dick told me, his approval of the highly satisfactory terms obtained. Anyone who had served with him would recognize this as entirely characteristic.

It was not less characteristic than the dignity of language and magnanimity of spirit with which he received the surrender in the Grand Harbour whose defence and relief had cost his fleet so many fine ships, aircraft and submarines and so many brave men. The famous signal, now preserved in the library at Windsor Castle, 'Be pleased to inform Their Lordships that the Italian battle fleet now lies at anchor under the guns of the fortress of Malta' is worthy of the occasion. His instructions to his own command that 'the Italian fleet having scrupulously honoured the engagement entered into by their Government, officers and ships' companies are to be treated with courtesy and consideration on all occasions' is worthy of the man.

* * *

A month after accepting the surrender Cunningham succeeded Pound as First Sea Lord. The death of Lady Pound in July had overborne the gallant fight her husband had put up against physical and nervous exhaustion. He sailed for the Quebec Conference in August but suffered a severe stroke soon after arrival and resigned on his return to England in September, dying a month later. Stephen Roskill's estimate of his great services in The War at Sea states the foundation of them with piercing clarity: 'He won the Prime Minister's confidence from the beginning and retained it to the last.'

Pound himself had repeatedly made it clear to Cunningham that he wished him to be his successor. The Prime Minister, however, remembering the forthrightness of the Commander-in-Chief Mediterranean in criticizing and even opposing projects which he considered ill-advised was anxious to avoid admitting so independent an officer to the highest councils of the war. He overrode his First Lord of the Admiralty, A. V. Alexander, who shared Pound's view that Cunningham was the obvious choice and offered the post to Bruce Fraser, Commander-in-Chief Home Fleet. Fraser declined in words that deserve to be remembered: that whereas he believed he had the confidence of his own fleet, 'Cunningham has that of the whole navy'. Even Churchill could hardly persist against such a weight of professional opinion. But he evidently put up a fight since Cunningham recorded in his diary two-and-a-half years later on 19 February 1946 a conversation with A. V. Alexander that has an authentic ring: 'Churchill was apparently frightened that my advent to the Admiralty would mean a very independent line and when finally consenting he said "You can have your Cunningham but if the Admiralty don't do as they are told I will bring down the Board in ruins even if it means my coming down with it." It's quite good to know that some of my signals from the Mediterranean went home.'

The ghost of Jacky Fisher had still not been laid. But Churchill had underestimated two qualities almost entirely lacking in Fisher with which Cunningham abounded, loyalty and reasonableness. Time and again in the diary which he began to keep after his first six months in office, he records his alarm or dismay at some proposed course of action that the Prime Minister was determined to drive through or some exposition of a question that was demonstrably at variance with the facts. But his reaction, however horrified, is always to try what patience and diplomacy and courtesy can do. Unlike Jacky he does not intrigue or threaten. If provoked by direct attack, especially if it is rude or sarcastic, he returns fire. His genius was of course for fighting and he undervalued himself as a member of the Chiefs of Staff Committee: 'one who was but an indifferent Staff Officer' as he described himself in a charming letter to Churchill accepting the honour which the Prime Minister offered him in terms of irresistible generosity at the end of the war with Germany. A truer estimate is made out in Alanbrooke's valediction of June 1946:

> We went through some very difficult days with Winston together and I could never have got through them without your help and staunch support.
>
> Then I should like to thank you for the wonderful cordial and friendly atmosphere which you engendered at all our meetings, your patience when listening to points of view you did not agree with and your constructive help throughout.

What made the post of First Sea Lord the most demanding of all the top service appointments was that the Admiralty, unlike the Air Ministry and the War Office, was both an administrative centre and an operational headquarters. The First Sea Lord was expected to run the navy as well as the naval side of the war, besides taking his place with his colleagues on the Chiefs of Staff Committee for the general direction and control of strategic policy. Manifestly it was impossible, particularly when the Prime Minister as Minister of Defence was by no means inclined to leave the last of these duties to his experts. To these commitments was added the necessity of maintaining the closest and friendliest relations both with the American Chiefs of Staff and the American navy.

Fortunately Cunningham's whole nature simplified his task. He was not interested in administration and when it was forced upon him showed himself hidebound and grudging. Unlike Jacky he had no wish to set the cat among the administrative pigeons and watch with amusement the outraged squawkings and flutterings that might ensue. As for the general conduct of the war at sea October 1943 was an auspicious moment. The battle on which everything depended, the Battle of the Atlantic, was going well. The

Mediterranean as Cunningham knew better than anyone else was now once again a route for warships and a base for offensive operations. Even the North Russian convoys could sail with a reasonable degree of safety after the sinking of the *Scharnhorst* at the end of the year. The main concern of the First Sea Lord was the preparation for the long awaited invasion of Europe's Atlantic coast and, at a further remove, the planning for a British contribution to the war in the Pacific once Germany had been defeated.

Eisenhower's appointment as Supreme Commander of the Anglo–American invasion naturally met with Cunningham's whole-hearted approval. 'He taught me how to be a King': George V's simple eloquent tribute to his secretary Lord Stamfordham might not inappositely be applied to their relationship. Certainly there were to be several occasions in the last eighteen months of the war when the value of the confidence Cunningham had given and received in this quarter was to be beyond measure. Not less to his satisfaction was Churchill's ready endorsement of his own candidate for the naval command of this vast Armada, Admiral Sir Bertram Ramsay.

To his other preoccupation, the planning and preparation of a British fleet to operate with the Americans in the Pacific, Mr Churchill was at first unresponsive and then hostile. Cunningham records that he first discussed it with the Prime Minister only a month after he had become First Sea Lord and they were both on passage in the *Renown* to the Cairo and Teheran conferences. 'Mr Churchill later forgot it, and for a very long time, nearly until a conference at Quebec in September 1944, refused to have anything to do with sending a fleet to the East, except to the East Indies. He required much persuasion.' This is the polite summary to be found in *A Sailor's Odyssey*. His diary shows that it was perhaps the most difficult single issue of his tenure of office.

Why were the two men so far apart on this issue? Partly it was the perennial difference of concern between politicians and pro-fessionals, the frocks and the brass as they were called in the First

World War. Churchill had not, as he himself pointed out, become His Majesty's First Minister to preside over the liquidation of the British Empire. His eyes were on the East Indies because it was there that great territories either directly colonial or under some form of British control had been seized by the Japanese and he wanted to make sure that when the Rising Sun came down the flagpole the Union Jack went up. To Cunningham this was a confusion of ends and means. When the Japanese were defeated the British would of course reoccupy their possessions. The point however was to employ the quickest and surest method of beating the Japanese in what was, overwhelmingly, a sea war. To engage and destroy the enemy's main force was by every professional tradition and theory the paramount objective. This was what the Americans were doing in the Pacific, which was the only place where it could be done. Unless Britain took part in this they would win the war on their own and would, quite legitimately, claim the victor's rights. Self-interest therefore demanded a strong British presence on the real field of battle, not the dissipation of force in sideshows. In any case it was a matter of honour. We had induced the Americans to treat the war against Hitler as the first priority on the clear understanding that once it was won we would support them with all our force against the Japanese who had originally attacked them. And beyond honour lay pride. The insulting contempt that Ernest J. King had shown towards the Royal Navy would have made a cooler tempered man than Cunningham determined that whether Ernie King liked it or not the White Ensign was going to fly in the great sea battles that were to be fought in the Pacific.

To much of this Mr Churchill was by temperament opposed. He was surprisingly ignorant of naval history and contemptuous of the strategic and tactical principles that might be learnt from its study. Hence, for instance, the preference, natural in an old cavalry officer, for dissipating anti-submarine forces in what he called 'hunter–killer' groups instead of employing them as convoy escorts, which might sound defensive but in fact offered far more chance of counter-offensive action. He looked at the sea with a land commander's eye, thrilling to the thought of capturing islands. Pantellaria had seemed to him an exciting and desirable objective in spite of the fact that it was useless as a harbour and had only a small airstrip while Malta which we were then holding on to with the greatest difficulty was a naval base of the first importance. Cunningham's opposition to this scheme, it will be remembered, had been grounded on such prosaic considerations. Now in the Indian Ocean the Prime Minister espied an islet just off Sabang, the northernmost port of Sumatra. If it were seized, would it not be ideal for the recapture of Singapore? The Chiefs of Staff unanimously supported Cunningham in scouting the idea. Fringe operations in war have the same appeal as fringe medicine in life. Part of it consists in getting away from the flat-footed obviousness of the professionals.

Cunningham summed up the frustrations thus imposed on several months of effort in a diary entry for 14 July 1944: 'The attitude of mind of the politicians about [anti-Japanese strategy] is astonishing. They are obviously frightened of the Americans laying down the law as to what is to happen when Japan is defeated to the various islands, ports, etc. This appears to be quite likely if the Americans are left to fight Japan by themselves.

'But they will not lift a finger to get a force into the Pacific. They prefer to hang about the outside and recapture our own rubber trees . . .'

His own position in this matter was a difficult one and was to become still more difficult, especially in the summer and autumn of 1944 as a combination of ill-health, exhaustion and the growing sense of forced consent to wrong decisions drove the Prime Minister into rages in which now the Americans, now his own Chiefs of Staff were held up to execration. In the end, as so often, it was Mr Churchill's very excesses of temperament that produced their own reaction and enabled wiser counsels to prevail.

At the beginning of 1944 with the Cairo and Teheran conferences behind him, Cunningham had settled into a course of life that was, with a few short intervals, to continue for the closing two years of his naval career. During the week he and his wife lived in a flat in the Admiralty looked after by a couple of Wrens. He liked to be in bed by eleven and at his desk again well before nine. He disapproved of the Whitehall system of opening for business at ten and drifting on till all hours. He particularly disliked the Prime Minister's habit of calling a meeting for ten at night which would not as a rule break up until well into the small hours. He detested the obligatory convivialities of parties and dinners chiefly because they wasted time for which he had urgent need but also on account of the demands made on a tender digestion. Living over the shop, with the Wrens to cook and clean, meant that the business of eating and sleeping could be regulated and reduced to essentials. On Saturday afternoons he could generally drive down with Lady Cunningham to Bishops Waltham, returning on the Sunday evening. While there he gardened doggedly and strenuously rather than joyously, chopped wood, cleared ditches and watched solicitously over the health of the dogs to which they were both devoted. Proximity to Portsmouth, and in the spring of '44 to the various headquarters involved in preparing for the invasion, enabled them to entertain in a private unostentatious way. As in Alexandria their hospitality was widely extended – to children of old friends and colleagues as well as to senior British and American officers, and much appreciated.

The London day began at nine with a survey of all current naval operations and a number of personal interviews to gain or impart up to the minute information. At ten-thirty the Chiefs of Staff Committee met and generally sat till one. After lunch he returned to his office where paperwork, meetings, interviews occupied him till dinner, after which he went back yet again for a final stint at his desk before turning in. On Monday evenings the Chiefs of Staff attended the regular Cabinet meeting to give an account of the progress of the war.

Of course this routine was often varied. The late night sessions with Mr Churchill and the War Cabinet have been too often described to require any setting of that scene. It was not one in which Cunningham shone, or desired to shine. He said as little as he could, determined at all costs to keep faith and maintain solidarity with his fellow Chiefs, to whom he could express dissent in the proper forum of their own committee. Towards the end of his time, after the war, he records in his diary (8 February 1946) taking the opportunity of a cocktail party to tell Tedder who had recently replaced Portal 'that it had been customary for the Chiefs of Staff to present a united front before Ministers and that he had attacked the navy twice. He apologised and we shall have no more of it.' When Churchill challenged him directly he felt bound to meet him even though the ground was not of his choosing, was indeed ground on which he knew himself to be at a disadvantage. The cut and thrust of Parliamentary debate gave seasoned politicians a comfortable supremacy over men who had been trained to decide and to act in a split second rather than to argue or to justify. None the less these long meetings did give him useful insight into the strengths and weaknesses of his political masters – and into none more than Churchill's.

The evidence of his diary is that by this stage in the war these meetings were apt to show the Prime Minister at his most difficult: rude, hectoring, violent, master neither of himself nor of the matter in hand, pouring out diatribes which were nothing to the purpose, unworthy of the speaker and embarrassing to his listeners. To cite but a few examples:

19 April 1944: The Egyptian crisis. The PM as usual out for the use of force regardless of the fact that the necessary force is not there. He also as usual said a few hard things about the local C-in-Cs.

6 July 1944: There is no doubt the PM was in no state to discuss anything. Very tired and too much alcohol. Meeting started unpropitiously by Brooke calling him to order for undermining Generals in command at Cabinet meetings by his criticisms. This obviously hurt him badly but he was in a terrible mood. Rude and sarcastic. I had a couple of blows up with him about the Far East.

The net result was that we sat from 22.00 to 01.45 listening to him talking mostly nonsense and got nowhere.

8 Aug 1944: No decisions were reached, in fact a thoroughly wasted day. What a drag on the wheel of war this man is. Everything is centralised in him with consequent indecision and waste of time.

On the next day Cunningham records with understandable fury the Prime Minister's resort to the childish stratagem of not circulating to the Chiefs of Staff until the actual meeting at half-past ten at night a paper that had been ready by four in the afternoon. 'Thus are we governed. I presume he himself has such a crooked mind that he is suspicious of the Chiefs of Staff . . .'

On 11 August things seemed to be moving to a crisis: 'In a closed session Ismay told us that he was just raving last night and absolutely unbalanced. He cannot get over not having had his way over Anvil [the invasion of the South of France championed by the Americans at the expense of the Italian campaign]. To my surprise it was Portal that suggested we should have to have a showdown with him before long if he went on as he is now. I have long thought it. He tries now to dictate to the Chiefs of Staff what they shall say to the US Chiefs of Staff.'

At this point, fortunately for everyone, the Prime Minister left for a visit to Italy. '14 August. Cabinet meeting at 17.30. Such a change with Atlee [A.B.C.'s invariable misspelling even when during the last year of his service he was the Prime Minister] in the chair. Everyone who wished to gave his opinion and yet business was expeditiously accomplished.'

A fortnight later Churchill returned not at all well. That Cunningham saw with perfect clarity the pros as well as the cons of serving under him appears in his entry for 29 August: 'It would be a tragedy if anything were to happen to him now. With all his faults (and he is the most infuriating man) he has done a great job for the country and besides there is no one else.'

The physical demands the Prime Minister made on himself over and above the fearful psychological strain to which at this stage of the war he was subject make it a matter for wonder that he retained the balance that he did. His own clear perception of the cold-blooded villainy that Stalin embodied, of the virulent malice which interpreted friendliness or generosity as timidity or weakness, was the more agonizing because Roosevelt in America and public opinion at home would have none of it. He could not afford to risk even the suspicion of a breach in the Grand Alliance. He knew that he and his country could make at best a scarcely honourable return for the courage and the trust shown by our Polish allies. And all this came on top of four years of running the war in the only way he knew how, a way that might be criticized as Cunningham had criticized it for want of delegation, but was inseparably now part of his style, part of himself. One cannot teach an old dog new tricks. And this old dog had for years defied every rule of canine health. He took no exercise. He spent hardly any time in the fresh air. He drank, ate and smoked with an Olympian contempt for consequences. Cunningham, who did none of these things, had himself made severe enough demands of an aging body and sympathetically ascribed the tantrums he recorded, however deplorable, to physical rather than moral causes.

It is not therefore surprising that when only a few days later the Prime Minister accompanied by the Chiefs of Staff sailed in the *Queen Mary* for the Quebec conference he should not be in his best form. 'In his worst mood,' Cunningham recorded on 8 September. '. . . Accusing the Chiefs of Staff of ganging up against him and keeping papers from him. The worst of it is his feeling against the Americans whom he accuses of doing the most awful things against the British. There is no question he is not well.' However, after a trying voyage, during which Mr Churchill attempted to order the Captain to change course so as to take the ship out of the warm sticky airstream he found so distressing, the conference went off better than Cunningham had feared. In spite of Mr Churchill's premonitory rumblings the offer of a British fleet to operate in the

Central Pacific was accepted by the President in plenary session. Best of all Ernie King's subsequent refusal to accept its services had to be openly retracted: 'In fact King made an ass of himself and having the rest of the US Chiefs of Staff against him had to give way . . . but with such a bad grace.'

The settling of this issue removed what had been a recurrent cause of contention. And with familiarity and the passage of time Cunningham came to a better understanding of, even a tolerant affection for, a great man in so many ways antipathetic to himself. In the following month when Churchill announced his imminent departure on yet another hazardous journey, this time to Moscow 'He told me that it was not necessary for me to come as I had no military knowledge. I replied that I had no wish to go but I preferred to put it that Stalin had no naval knowledge. He didn't mean to be rude but just was.'

By January 1945 philosophical acceptance of the Prime Minister's perversities had shown Cunningham how to overcome them:

6 January: informed by telephone that the PM has refused to agree to the appointment of Harold Burrough to relieve Ramsay [who had been killed in an aircrash] on the ground that the post could now be abolished and the staff saved.

How he works in such complete ignorance and disregard for facts beats me.

8 Jan [about midnight]: Went over and saw the PM. He consented at once to Burrough's appointment.

Three months later the note of wisdom and tolerance is even stronger.

12 April: It is curious that with all his great qualities when he deals with personalities he gets childish. He is such a bad picker too.

13 April: The First Lord being away I had an interview by myself with the PM on the subject of his minute ordering trawlers to be given up [i.e. released from mine-sweeping duties, etc. to return to fishing]. I was quite firm with him but persuasive . . . As usual when one gets alongside him on a subject he knows little about I had my way. I was glad the First Lord was not there. He rather gets the PM's back up and he enjoys bullying him.

* * *

Cunningham's relations with the Prime Minister have been given pride of place because to a greater or lesser degree they set limits to whatever he could achieve in each of the many fields of activity for which as First Sea Lord he was responsible. Manifestly the same is true, if not truer, over the general conduct of affairs on which the Chiefs of Staff advised the government.

Of his naval responsibilities at the beginning of 1944 unquestionably the most important were the preparations for Overlord (the invasion of France) and the defence of our Atlantic convoys against the U-boats. Cunningham's special relationship with General Eisenhower and the brilliant work of his colleague in the Sicilian invasion, Admiral Ramsay, largely relieved him of anxiety about the naval side of Overlord. At any rate there is very little about it in his diary. As to the Battle of the Atlantic he inherited a first-class organization and command structure to which he pays generous tribute in his autobiography. The question that gave him far the most difficulty, that of sending a British fleet to the Pacific, has already been discussed. The other great issue which occupied the Chiefs of Staff and obsessed the Prime Minister was that of Operation Anvil (the invasion of the South of France).

There all day long the noise of battle rolled. But as Cunningham himself makes clear in *A Sailor's Odyssey* he played no important part in it, simply supporting his fellow Chiefs when the Staff view was called for. Anvil was very much an American project. Both the US administration and the US Chiefs of Staff had pressed hard for an assault on the Atlantic coast of Europe in 1943. Having given way to their British allies over this by accepting the attack on North Africa and the subsequent invasion of Sicily and Italy they were determined to stick out for Anvil as a follow-through for Overlord. The landing craft and assault ships required would have to be taken from what would otherwise have been available for the Italian campaign and, further afield, from those provisionally assigned to South East Asia Command for operations against the Japanese in Burma and Malaya. Both of these were close to Mr Churchill's heart. The British Chiefs of Staff on the whole supported him but were readier than he to concede the weight of the military argument that Anvil concentrated Allied forces against the main force of the principal enemy instead of dissipating them. Cunningham seems privately to have accepted this as the correct application of the principles of war but to have felt, surely rightly, that the matter was one for soldiers rather than sailors to settle.

Cunningham's diary suggests the Italian campaign held its high place in the Prime Minister's priorities at least in part on account of the British general in command. Field Marshal Alexander had incurred Cunningham's hostility at the time of the Salerno landings for improper interference in affairs that clearly lay within the naval commander's competence and for allowing his chief subordinate, Montgomery, to give out that the navy was holding up the progress of the campaign. The letter he wrote him on 26 August 1943 is one of the fiercest to be found in his papers. On the other hand Alexander seemed to enjoy an unlimited lease of the Prime Minister's confidence. As late as 12 April 1945 Cunningham noted: 'Montgomery he has fairly well sized up but he is completely bluffed by Alexander.' Churchill had wanted to make him Supreme Commander in the Mediterranean as long ago as the Cairo conference in November 1943 but had been baulked by the united opposition of the Chiefs of Staff. A year later the death of Sir John Dill resulted in the transfer of Field Marshal

'Jumbo' Wilson from Italy to Washington as his relief. 'Of course the only reason for this is to get Wilson out of the way and appoint Alexander Supreme Commander Mediterranean – a post for which he is totally unfitted', wrote Cunningham on 4 November, adding two days later: 'All three Chiefs of Staff realise that this would be a bad appointment. The CIGS hesitates to tell the Prime Minister so as he is accused of jealousy.' A point of principle was involved: the Prime Minister was overriding his professional advisers on a professional, not a political, matter. On 7 November at the Staff meeting with Churchill Cunningham put forward his objections to the proposed appointment. 'These were received calmly by the PM who merely said he recognised my right through knowledge of the personalities to criticize the appointment but that he disagreed with me . . . The tragedy is that the CAS and CIGS agree with me but decided to take the line of least resistance.'

The issue roused him deeply. Next day at the Chiefs of Staff meeting 'I pointed out the inherent dishonesty of the whole transaction – the signal to the US cracking up Wilson and the PM's remarks last night running him down. My colleagues appeared to be a little shamefaced. CIGS made a half-hearted semi-apology and CAS said he agreed with everything I had said . . .' A week later, on 15 November, at a Chiefs of Staff meeting

It came out that the PM was carrying on a signal correspondence with Alexander behind Wilson's back and in his [i.e. Alexander's] signals to the PM criticising Wilson's set up.

I was almost too disgusted to speak. Portal came out with that it showed Alex's complete unfitness for the post of SC. It is all so dishonest . . .

I am disgusted over the state of impotence the CoS Committee is reduced to. Here we are – all three of us know that Alexander is unfitted to be SC Med. and yet we are allowing ourselves to be bullied into it by the PM.

Perhaps no passage illustrates more clearly the contrast between Cunningham's cast of mind and Fisher's. Fisher would have been, was, equally outraged by Churchill's overriding the considered assessment of his service advisers of a service question. But the moral obliquity of going behind the back of a man to whom you were bound in a relation of mutual trust would not have worried him in the least. It was exactly what he was accustomed to doing himself. He could have cited maxims from the ancient world, from Macchiavelli, from almost every age in his support. But he could not personify as Cunningham did the simplicity, the straightforwardness, that is so compelling a part of the ideal naval character.

With Montgomery Cunningham's relations were barbed but not embittered. Both men were pugnacious by temper. Montgomery had early incurred Cunningham's wrath in North Africa by unfounded accusations of naval dilatoriness in clearing captured harbours. During the operations against Sicily he overstepped the line dividing naval from military responsibility and was sharply rapped over the knuckles. It was not to be expected that he would modify his conduct in the exciting summer of 1944. In July he complained to the Chiefs of Staff that Cherbourg was not being cleared fast enough. Cunningham refuted this at a meeting on the 15th. 'CIGS took it very well and gave me his opinion of Montgomery which approximates closely to my own.' In November Monty enlisted Churchill's support for removing Admiral Ramsay from Eisenhower's headquarters. This arose directly from Montgomery's dissatisfaction with the value of the capture of Antwerp, an objective in which he had disregarded the repeated warnings of both Cunningham and Ramsay that a port 30 miles up an estuary is useless until the estuary itself is clear. On 4 October Cunningham had summarized Ramsay's account before the Chiefs of Staff: 'The fact appears to be that Montgomery has not given the clearing of the estuary of the Schelt [sic] the attention it should have had and Ike though realising the urgency has not succeeded in compelling Montgomery. Well, they will and are paying for it by the slowing or even halting of our advance . . . An outstanding case of not putting first things first.' Two days later the Chiefs heard the point driven home: 'Bertie Ramsay did some straight talking about Montgomery's failure to clear the estuary of the Scheldt. Eisenhower apparently took the blame on himself. He would. But the fact remains that the whole army is stuck due to not having captured a port close enough to the front line . . . It is extraordinary that the generals will pay no attention to our warnings.' Ramsay in fact retained the appointment which he had discharged with such conspicuous success until his death in an aircrash in the following January.

The two men continued to keep a sharp eye on each other. Cunningham's excellent relations with the American generals from Eisenhower down enabled him to throw his weight into the scale when Montgomery's vanity and tactlessness threatened to upset the delicate balance of the Alliance. When the war against Germany was won, Montgomery took it upon himself to order the naval forces in North West Europe to splice the mainbrace. Cunningham's rebuke earned the rare tribute of an apology: '. . . in my ignorance I did not know that this was reserved for the King'. A month later at the Potsdam Conference he came to lunch at Cunningham's quarters '. . . and was quite interesting. I noted he called me "Sir". A new departure, perhaps intended to placate.' They never became friends but when in January 1946 Montgomery took his seat in the Lords he asked Cunningham as a sailor and Trenchard as an airman to act as his supporters.

With the airmen he had correct if cool relations. Tedder he knew from long service together but neither liked nor trusted. 'Bomber' Harris he met at Chequers and took an instant dislike to, but their paths did not cross. Sholto Douglas at Coastal Command he conceded in his diary on 21 June 1945 'has done well with us on the whole. He is I think not clever enough to be underhand.' Portal, his colleague as Chief of Staff, he had known and liked from their days at the Imperial Defence College. He respected him for his professional knowledge and for his obvious abilities and sobriety of judgement. He sometimes thought that he lacked the courage of his convictions and felt, probably with reason, that he was more adroit in his handling of matters that might affect the future interests of the two services than he was. The bruises from the inter-service jousts of the twenties and thirties were still tender. With the end of the second war coming into sight a First Sea Lord had to keep a sharp look-out. In December 1944 Cunningham was in two minds over a proposal that the RAF should be put in charge of future aircraft production: 'The truth is the Navy mistrusts deeply the RAF with reason! But are we without sin?' But on the next day he had a frank talk with Portal and gave preliminary assent. 'I think we are doing right taking the long view. We do not want eternal friction between the services.'

What were his relations with his own Commanders-in-Chief? On the whole very good, but by no means invariably so. Harwood whom he had thought inadequate to relieve him at Alexandria in 1942 had himself been relieved early in 1943 and replaced by Sir John Cunningham, of whom A.B.C. had a high opinion and with whom, in spite of marked differences of temperament, he got on extremely well. This seems not to be true of the holder of the most important command of all, Admiral Sir Max Horton, who was responsible for fighting the U-boats in the Atlantic. Horton's conduct of the campaign from 1942 to the end of the war was magnificent: but in the whole of *A Sailor's Odyssey* there are only two coldly perfunctory references to him, whereas the work of two of his subordinates Admiral Sir John Edelsten at the Admiralty and the distinguished lawyer Rodger Winn in the Submarine Tracking Room is generously recognized. Stephen Roskill points out in *Churchill and the Admirals* that Cunningham prevented Horton's career from being crowned with the peacetime command of one of the three home ports, an honour richly deserved. A diary entry records a contentious interview with him on a private matter (unspecified). Old loyalties and old enmities clouded Cunningham's professional judgement. As has been said, even his admirers attributed the sinking of the *Valiant* and the *Queen Elizabeth* in Alexandria harbour to his retention of an incompetent officer in charge of the boom defence for the sake of auld lang syne.

This trait perhaps had positive value in his dealings with his old friend and term-mate Sir James Somerville during his command of the Eastern Fleet. Somerville's squabbles with Mountbatten, far his junior on the Navy List but his superior as Supreme Commander South East Asia, have been described by Philip Ziegler with admirable fairness.* Cunningham certainly resented Mountbatten's itch to extend his already head-turning authority. 'I wish that young man would mind his own business,' he exploded to himself on 31 August 1944 on being told by the Chancellor of the Exchequer that he had Mountbatten's authority for saying that servicemen did not want a rise in pay but would prefer an increased gratuity. None the less he resisted the efforts of both parties to involve the Chiefs of Staff in their unseemly wrangling over pecking-order pettinesses. When he did finally have to give judgement on appeal he did not allow old friendship or fresh irritation to distort it. But his relationship with Somerville certainly made it easier for the older man to reconcile himself to a ruling he might otherwise have resented.

Somerville was relieved in the autumn of 1944 by the admiral with whom Cunningham's relations are much the most interesting, Bruce Fraser. It will be remembered that Churchill had offered him the post of First Sea Lord in preference to A.B.C. As Commander-in-Chief Home Fleet he scored two brilliant successes: the sinking of the *Scharnhorst* at the end of December 1943 and the attack by carrier-borne aircraft on the *Tirpitz* at her heavily protected moorings in Kaa Fiord early in April 1944. The planning and execution of this extremely hazardous operation in Arctic waters deserved and won the highest praise. But though a large number of hits had been scored and the casualties aboard the *Tirpitz* had been heavy it was soon evident that she had only been put out of action for a few months, not damaged beyond repair. Cunningham at once ordered the Commander-in-Chief to repeat the attack at the earliest possible moment. To his astonishment Fraser flatly refused. He

Mountbatten (1985), pp. 231–40. The author quotes the judgement of Somerville's secretary: 'In fact they both behaved like schoolgirls at times'.

pointed out that the success of the operation had been achieved by an unrepeatable combination of elements: surprise, the fact that a large convoy to Russia had drawn off the attention of enemy submarines and most important of all, the choice of that narrow band on the meteorological pattern when the nights were long enough to bring so large a force within striking distance undetected and yet not so low in temperature as to make flying off and on impracticable.

Cunningham himself had spent the weekend after the attack at Chequers. 'Had a shave in cold water. It's time they renovated and brought up to date that Chequers House. Running water in the bedrooms would make all the difference.' Back in London he had a real row with Fraser over the telephone 'in a most truculent and obstinate mood'. He refused to repeat the operation, 'in fact indicated that he would haul his flag down if ordered to repeat it. I told him to sleep on it and call me up in the morning.' On the next day, 14 April, 'I understood him to acquiesce.' But wrongly. Considerable diplomacy was needed to reach a compromise by which Fraser agreed to detach appropriate forces at the first suitable opportunity with an attack on the *Tirpitz* as one of two alternative objectives if conditions permitted. Such an opportunity did occur but a change in weather rendered the attack impossible and the second alternative was taken. No further opportunity presented itself.

Fraser's behaviour, it may strike the reader, was nothing if not Cunninghamesque. He was the Commander-in-Chief, the man on the spot. He was charged with certain objectives and entrusted with certain forces to attain them. How best to achieve these ends was for him to judge. If his superiors did not think him sufficiently eager to get at the enemy they should replace him. No doubt Cunningham was uneasily aware that this position was exactly that which he himself had maintained and, if so circumstanced, would maintain again. What made it all the more vexing was that Fraser was his own choice for command of the British Pacific fleet which against the open hostility of Ernie King and the subtler obstructiveness of

Churchill he was labouring to establish. Finally there was no arguing with Fraser's record. As a Commander-in-Chief of a fleet it was second only to his own.

The two sides of his nature are well illustrated in his reactions. The tendency, noted by Admiral Godfrey, to shout and bully when demonstrably worsted in argument can be discerned in his private reflections, recorded in his diary. In late November he was enraged by a letter from Fraser, then on the point of hoisting his flag over the Pacific Fleet, complaining of the Admiralty's negative attitude towards all his proposals and suggesting that they had better relieve him. 'I am in doubt myself whether he is the man for the job the way he has behaved lately.' A week later his temper was still ruffled. 'I confess I do not understand Fraser. There is no urgent desire to get to the scene of action. It may be the climate but there has been dilatoriness in all his dealings.' The cause of the trouble was briefly that in the Pacific the navy faced problems of supply and administration utterly different from any previous experience. Campaigns were fought thousands of miles from the nearest naval base. To keep ships in a proper state of fighting efficiency required an enormous fleet train of vessels. No doubt such necessities ran the risk of being classed as Rolls-Royce and velvet-arsed.

That Bruce Fraser, whom those who served under him remember as a gentle, modest, avuncular figure, should have stood up to Cunningham at his fiercest adds a certain piquancy to the relationship. But the other side of Cunningham's nature should not be forgotten. He was capable, as his relations with the Americans show, of tact and charm and patience. He was passionately loyal. And in his heart of hearts he, in marked contrast to Jacky Fisher, liked being stood up to. 'I hate staff officers who agree with me.'

Not all the business of the First Sea Lord or of the Chiefs of Staff was so challenging. What attitude ought their Lordships to take towards the maisons de tolerance in Alexandria? Sir John Cunningham, the Commander-in-Chief, was 'much in favour' of them. But the Board took the view, perhaps with regret, that 'when the various societies are after us it could not be defended.' That decision at least did not take long. Unlike the question, hardly more serious, which came up that same autumn of 1944, namely whether or not there should still be a Commander-in-Chief Ceylon and if so who should it be. The Chiefs of Staff were ready to scrap it. The emergency for which the command had been created was long over. There was already quite enough top brass in South East Asia. But the Colonial Office dug in its toes. Wearily, the Chiefs agreed on a nomination, only to find that their man had just been designated Governor-General of Southern Rhodesia.

A more immediate impact on their deliberations was made by the Flying Bombs. Inability to mount any effective defence against these alarming weapons left reprisals as the sole countermeasure. Cunningham, on 1 July, suggested the bombing of small, and thus presumably undefended, German towns. Churchill accepted the idea with enthusiasm but said that he must be provided with 'some excuse such as making parts of the machine, otherwise he will be right up against J.C. as exemplified by the Archbishop of Canterbury'. Two days later the proposal was again discussed. The Chief of Air Staff was 'very hot against it on the grounds that it would be improperly diverting the bombing effort. The Secretary of State for Air said pilots engaged on bombing Hun small towns would be shot if captured. There may be some truth in this and only stresses what a careful examination must be made before a decision is reached.'

It was this sobering professionalism that was to prove decisive. Retaliation by the use of poison gas was next considered but by the end of the month the Prime Minister minuted that 'he could do nothing if the warriors as well as the parsons were against him'. None the less the Chiefs were, understandably, rattled by the effect of the bombs and, on 14 August, at a Cabinet meeting presided over by Attlee put forward the palliative of deception. The Germans were to be led to believe, by feeding false reports through agents, that the bombs were falling to the north of London so that they might be induced to divert them further south and thus reduce casualties. This, Cunningham records, was consistently opposed by the politicians. 'One should not interfere with the Almighty's decrees by killing others than those He intends.'

An even more serious threat was the development of U-boats capable of high speed under water and equipped with Schnorkel that enabled them to stay submerged pretty well indefinitely. Coupled with the development of high-speed Morse transmission this could have disarmed the techniques by which victory in the Battle of the Atlantic had been won and which had been employed with such devastating success in carrying troops and supplies across the Channel. Cunningham, against his usual cult of the Silent Service, had been pleased to find Churchill, on his return from France on 24 July, 'much inclined to publicise the work of the Escort Groups and Coastal Command in keeping the invasion passage clear of submarine attack. The President has however rather forbidden it. I do not wish to speak ill of anyone but this is a noteworthy all British success and I fear the President's message has been put up by the Navy Department.' By the end of the year however he was up against more formidable opposition than the spite of Fleet Admiral Ernest J. King. On Christmas Eve a transport was sunk off Cherbourg with the loss of 800 lives. The new types of U-boat were being produced in such numbers that only the bombing of the yards and bases and the advance of the Allied armies into Germany prevented a serious setback in the war at sea.

On the public side of a First Sea Lord's duties Cunningham's score was not high. The prospect of making a speech filled him with dismay; the preparations took up a quite disproportionate amount of his time and energy: the results rarely, by his own account, justified the sacrifice. Worst of all to him was the necessity of speaking *ex tempore*. At a Board of Admiralty dinner to celebrate the Prime Minister's seventieth birthday Churchill suddenly proposed his health. At the Trafalgar Night dinner at Chatham Barracks, a meal for which the mess caterer should have been decorated on the spot, Jack Tovey called his brother officers to their feet 'in a rather fulsome and very flattering proposal of my health'. Consciousness of his own inadequacy in reply is painfully recorded.

These were naval occasions where if he did not feel at ease at least he felt at home. To be exposed to this kind of thing in unfamiliar surroundings was a more severe trial. Nothing but a sense of duty could have carried him through.

Obstinate in so many ways he seems to have accepted against his own principles and personal taste the need for at least some publicity for the navy. In July 1944 as we have seen he resented its denial through the supposed malice of Ernie King. Yet on 30 August he was arguing the direct opposite with the press baron, Lord Camrose. 'The greatest compliment that could be paid to the Navy was that it should be taken for granted and that so long as those that mattered knew the truth I was content.' One cannot imagine Jacky Fisher making so elementary a political misjudgement. When the war had ended and honours and rewards were being handed out Cunningham was enraged by the meagre proportion allotted to the navy. Its achievements had indeed been taken for granted. On the other hand three months after his argument with Camrose we find him agreeing with his colleagues on the Board that more publicity for the navy is urgently needed. 'Bruntisfield [the Parliamentary Secretary] said it would take about 80 officers. Well, they must be found.'

Public recognition, in spite of his own unobtrusiveness, was most imaginatively granted him by Churchill in recommending him to the King for the Order of the Thistle. No honour, and he received many, gave him so much pleasure. A month later he accompanied the Prime Minister and the other Chiefs of Staff to Yalta, where for once he made a speech which even by his own self-deprecating account seems to have gone down well. It was the first time he had met the Russians. He was not impressed by his naval opposite number. Stalin he found 'good and clear in his points, the PM also very good.' That is about as far as one gets with A.B.C. at these exotic gatherings that cry out for a Creevy or a Greville, a Harold Nicolson or a Chips Channon, to sketch from the life. At Potsdam later in the year his digestion made the whole proceedings a test of survival. But even at Yalta the large and by no means appetizing meals of unfamiliar food accompanied and followed by innumerable toasts were taxing enough. Less demanding but hardly more enjoyable were the domestic social obligations of his post. A dinner given by the First Lord, A. V. Alexander, on 2 January 1945 may be taken as a sample. Remarking that it was a queer party, full of rich business people, he jots down a few names and impressions: 'Frank Reynolds [probably a mistake for Frank Owen], Mountbatten's publicity expert and his wife, an ex-cabaret artist, Mrs Hartman, has a lot to do with General Motors and farms in Wiltshire, Mrs Gasket, something to do with somebody's tinned peas, or had as she has now sold them to Leverhulme for a million. Not a very exciting evening. One finds oneself out of touch, and the First Lord treats one as a sort of exhibit.'

The last eighteen months of Cunningham's service – he left the Admiralty in June 1946 – round off his career, rising to no climax and offering little fresh insight into his character. It was entirely right that he should have been the professional head of the navy at the moment of victory in a war that he had done so much to win. As a First Sea Lord he was an alert, infinitely experienced officer of the watch rather than an originator or an inspirer. When a crisis arose his reactions were characterized by promptness, steadiness and common sense.

This was exemplified in June 1945 when De Gaulle's suspicion of British intentions towards Syria and Lebanon and Churchill's alarmed distrust of the General's wilder flights might have had serious consequences. On 5 June the French cruiser *Jeanne d'Arc* was reported to have embarked troops, supposedly for the Levant, and to be sailing eastwards. Churchill sent Cunningham a message suggesting her interception at sea 'saying that perhaps there would be less bloodshed this way. I doubt it. There are plenty of forces available to intercept her but I think that very tricky quality French honour would demand that she be sunk rather than yield to force. Have told John Cunningham to get the *Anson* [a modern battleship] out if possible. That anyway will produce the overwhelming force necessary to assuage French honour.

. . . Cabinet at 18.00. PM very unsound on the question of intercepting the *Jeanne d'Arc*. Suggesting that a ship should steam alongside her and tell her not to go to Beirut but was not to use force if she disobeyed. A fantastic idea.' Fortunately the following day brought a report that the ship had disembarked her troops at Bizerta and had resumed her passage.

In such situations Cunningham's good sense could be relied on. But when, as victory drew closer, questions of future defence policy or the development of new techniques of naval warfare were to be considered there was none of Fisher's boldness or imagination. If Fisher was sometimes silly and often unstable Cunningham was safe and stodgy. Comparisons of this kind are no doubt always unfair. Cunningham had the responsibility for the day to day conduct of the most extensive naval war in which the country had ever been engaged and, for the last nine months, for clearing up after it. He was aging and tiring. Both his trouble with his right eye and with his stomach put him in the surgeon's hands. By the time he left the Admiralty he was having 'what the medicos call some embarrassment' with his heart.

The ending of the war with Germany meant the end of the Churchill coalition. Cunningham had enjoyed at least correct relations with the ministers with whom he had to deal except for Lord Leathers, the Minister of War Transport, who rarely appears in his diary without some disobliging description. The formation of the caretaker adminstration was announced on 26 May. 'I see we are after all to have Brendan Bracken as First Lord. I hope only temporarily, I dislike him and he is Winston's creature and this is obviously W.'s way of trying to gain closer control of the Admiralty. At the same time he is not afraid of standing up for his Department. He hates James Grigg [Secretary of State for War] so there may be wigs on the green over the manpower . . . But I dislike all these politicians. . .'

The return of the Labour Government brought the return of A. V. Alexander under whom Cunningham found no difficulty in serving, except for his itch to interfere in matters outside his proper field.

Most unwisely Alexander attempted to obtain the promotion of a particular officer who had been passed over. 'I had to be very firm with him and asked him if he really thought he knew more about the question than the Sea Lords. Such a pity with his juniors on the political scene present as he was of course completely defeated.' (21 December 1945.) Ten days later Cunningham was infuriated at his having lent the Painted Hall at Greenwich for the entertainment of UNO. But in general they jogged on together well enough.

In any case A.B.C. knew that his work was done. On 10 August, the day he heard that the Japanese had accepted the terms of surrender, he wrote in his diary 'Well it looks like being all over for which we must be profoundly thankful ... I do not wish to hang on here keeping other people back, so as soon as the fleet gets a bit sorted out I will go. My relief requires thought.'

A day earlier he had received 'a charming letter from Winston offering me a barony as a recognition of the work of his friends the Chiefs of Staff during the time he was PM. I fear it is just what I don't want. I have not the cash to sustain the dignity. CIGS feels the same but after consultation we decided we could not refuse when offered in such generous terms.'

This was the opening bid in the negotiations over honours and rewards. In Cunningham's view there were two cardinal points at issue: first, the just allotment of whatever was on offer between the three fighting services; and second, the maintenance of the traditional cash rewards to the principal fighting commanders. These he clearly looked on as something that had been earned, as distinct from any honours which came as it were *ex gratia* rather than as of right. Serving officers in the nature of things had to make financial sacrifices that civil servants and politicians as a rule did not. They often had to maintain two homes, to go abroad at a moment's notice often for long and always for indeterminate periods and were thus effectively disabled from any management of their own affairs. The gold boxes and magnificent gifts of plate which the city merchants showered on the commanders of Nelson's day were both expressions of national gratitude and payment for substantial services rendered. Prize money was another recognition of the debt the country owed its senior commanders. Although it had been paid at the end of the war of 1914–18 it was trivial by the standards of the French wars. The difference had been to some extent made good by the payment of large gratuities and it was these that Cunningham, who was neither rich nor avaricious, wished to secure. Though uninterested in peerages himself he regarded such honours as direct public recognition of what the navy had achieved. At the same time he felt, as the passage quoted makes plain, that a peer if he were not to bring ridicule on his order ought to live in a certain style.

On the question of money he was defeated. He fought long and hard, driven both by a conviction that he and his fellows were being denied fair play and that, as he noted on 10 December 1945, it would 'make the difference between a penurious and a comfortable old age. We will have to give up Palace House . . .' This worry persisted through the early days of his retirement and weighed largely with him in considering the approach made early in 1946 by Sir Alan Lascelles, the King's private secretary, as to becoming Governor-General of Australia. 'I do not want to land myself in the poor-house,' he wrote in the notably reluctant reply he drafted on 4 March. It was a post for which he felt neither enthusiasm nor aptitude, though both a recognition of the honour done him and the habit of duty to the Crown forbade turning it down out of hand. Lord Gowrie, a previous Governor-General, assured him that it was possible to do the job properly without being out of pocket. But in April Cunningham was in hospital for some weeks with a heart complaint. On 14 August, no doubt with relief, he declined for the second time – the King had asked him to reconsider his earlier refusal – on grounds of health.

The offer, a personal rather than a service honour, was naturally not made public. But Cunningham, the last man to put himself forward, was vigilant on the navy's behalf. As early as 25 October he records a telephone conversation with Churchill, ostensibly about some other matter. 'I think he has a guilty conscience about the Navy. Curiously he said that in his Alamein dinner speech he had tried to hold the balance even between the services ... according to press reports he never mentioned the Air or the Navy. Nor did Montgomery, but that is only to be expected of him. It's wonderful how the Army wins the war by itself.' By the end of November he was expressing his outrage at the disproportion in the proposed distribution of honours. On 4 December, after consulting Geoffrey Blake, he refused to accept the Viscountcy offered him if the lack of recognition of his fellow sailors was the Prime Minister's last word. Next day Attlee gave ground. Both Tovey and Fraser were to receive baronies. Mountbatten, too, was to be made a baron on the navy list. 'I repudiated this absolutely, pointing out that MB had not been made a Supreme Commander because of his abilities as a naval commander but for political reasons. I refused to commit myself to withdrawing from the stand I had taken up until I had considered the new situation.

Then came what was to me the astonishing offer of an earldom for myself. I have told the man (A.V.A.) time and again that I care nothing for these honours for myself and he evidently doesn't believe me. It's rather humiliating . . .'

It was a ding-dong battle. Amongst possibilities for a compromise Cunningham had suggested that some of the commanders whom Attlee was unwilling to ennoble (and one must remember that this was before the introduction of life peerages) might be rewarded with baronetcies. On 7 December he records '1st Lord told me that the PM had now come round on the question of baronetcies but I have a feeling that he is again going to weigh the scales against the Navy.' On the 10th Alexander told him that the Prime Minister had gone back on his decision about baronetcies and was now offering a barony to Tovey and nothing to James Somerville. Reluctantly Cunningham reckoned that this was the best he could do for his friends and colleagues. Tovey and he accepted on the 11th a barony and a viscountcy respectively. 'I don't want it. I am too poor for it to be of any use to me.' But 'for the good of the navy one must take it.'

Cunningham was surely right in perceiving a steady bias in favour of the army in the assignment of post-war honours as in the selection during the war of Supreme Commanders. Mountbatten, the only naval officer to hold such an appointment, was, as Cunningham quite fairly pointed out, not chosen for his eminence in that profession. 'The PM has gone all Army - neither of the other two services mean anything to him at the moment and I think he looks on all admirals as half-wits – it may be that he knows they are mostly independent-minded' he had burst out in a letter to Somerville on 28 November 1944. The leading figures in government, Churchill, Attlee, Eden, even second-rank cabinet ministers such as Dalton, Duff Cooper, Macmillan and Lyttelton, had all served in the army in their formative years. It is not necessary to share Cunningham's opinion of Field Marshal Alexander ('The man's a mountebank') to feel that his viscountcy* added to that conferred on Montgomery did disturb the balance between the services.

Every aspect of Cunningham's own character and mentality can be discerned in this struggle. His passionate loyalty to the officers who had served with him, his distrust of politicians, his genuine lack of interest in social rank, his tenacity, his sense of fair play limited though it might be by his strong prejudices. Vian, whom Cunningham liked and admired, had been knighted for a fighting record whose brilliance and daring had not been surpassed but received no further recognition. It seems a missed opportunity. Max Horton received the GCB which hardly did justice to his outstanding services. Cunningham's want of impartiality in this case has already been mentioned. But what is beyond dispute is his own selflessness.

He was true to his intention to vacate his office as soon as he had made satisfactory arrangements for the succession. On New Year's Day 1946 he saw the First Lord and asked him to approach the Prime Minister on the matter, suggesting the name of Sir John

*He was advanced to an earldom in 1952 for his distinguished service as Governor-General of Canada.

Cunningham. He heard that evening that Attlee had agreed and the appointment was duly announced on 1 March. He was glad to be going. The emotional and intellectual strain of six years of the highest responsibility had been enormous. No wonder his body was beginning to creak under it. 'I am enjoying an empty mind,' he wrote to Admiral J. H. Godfrey, 'It has been so overflowing these last two or three years and can do with a rest.' This feeling was intensified by the consciousness that there were battles still to be fought which required fresh energy. 'A perfectly frightful memo by the PM' he recorded on 25 February. 'Thoroughly defeatist and suggesting that we should abandon all our interests in the Mediterranean as we could not hope to keep it open in wartime. Such reading of history. Well I hope the Chiefs of Staff will take a strong line. I will urge them to it.' Ten days later, reflecting on the offer of the Australian Governor-Generalship, he concludes 'I want a rest but after a short time doing nothing I feel I should get very restive and impossible to live with. Perhaps I can still be of some little value to the Empire.'

By the following month he was in Haslar hospital. A seaman who had served with him in *Scorpion* from 1913 to 1916 saw the news and wrote to wish him well. His papers contain many such letters, habitually answered in his own hand, usually occasioned by his name appearing in the newspapers. By his standards such recognition was more valuable than the laurels for which he saw the world contending.

Not that these were absent. On 4 February he had had a note informing him that Marshal Juin wished to present him with the Grand Cross of the Legion of Honour on his impending visit to London. Cunningham tactfully informed the French authorities that General Giraud had given it to him three years earlier. The mistake in their records was admitted and the Médaille Militaire was handsomely substituted. Cunningham took the opportunity of the official lunch at the Savoy on the 12th to ask the French admiral sitting next to him about his old friend Esteva and was somewhat reassured. 'I think the French Navy are all very sad about him and I gather he is not being harshly treated.'

Cunningham was not the man to forget old friends. In his retirement he continued to exchange letters with Esteva. His good opinion was evidently a great source of strength in his misfortunes. Such friendship warmly given was warmly returned. No letters to A.B.C. are more generous or more genuine than those with which Eisenhower congratulated him on every mark of public recognition. On his barony in Churchill's resignation honours Ike had written 'You well know that in my conviction there is no award, however great, that can ever symbolize the debt owed you by the United Nations.' Ike always remembered his birthday and on one occasion offered him the free use of the flat in Culzean Castle which he had been given for his lifetime but was not then able to avail himself of.

A.B.C.'s fears that he might decline into an irritable restlessness were not realized. He was much in demand. Only the day after his decoration by Marshal Juin he was invited to become Head of the British Legion. His refusal was prompt. 'The Legion is too political, the sailors have no use for it.' And what would he use for income? Fortunately aptitude and opportunity coincided. The reading public's appetite for wartime memoirs was insatiable and some redress for governmental meanness could be obtained from publishers. There was in any case an official history to be written on which he would be much consulted, despatches to be published in the *London Gazette* which could not in the nature of things have appeared during the actual course of the war. The historian's function as Cunningham had always appreciated is by no means exclusively academic. It was ignorance of history that had cost the country dear in two world wars. It was to history that Cunningham was instinctively ready to appeal, as can be seen from his immediate reaction to Attlee's memorandum on defence already quoted.

At lunch in Downing Street in November 1944 Churchill had declared that history would pronounce on the invasion of the French Mediterranean coast 'and rather implied that the verdict would be unfavourable. I suggested that it would depend on who wrote the history. To which the Prime Minister replied that he intended to have a hand in that.' The volumes of *The Second World War* soon began to make the claim good. In October 1949 Churchill's principal historical assistant G. R. G. Allen, preparing for the publication of volume iii, sent Cunningham the final draft of 'the passages that affect you' so that he might raise any objections he might have. Since he was already at work on his own memoirs he knew that he was sure of a hearing for his own side of the story where it differed from Churchill's. But the draft account of the pressure brought on him over the episode of the *Barham* and the bombardment of Tripoli (see pp.113–15) seemed to him both disingenuous in itself and to impute that quality to Dudley Pound. The version submitted to him apparently suggested that the idea of sinking the *Barham* was thought up by Pound as a trick to induce the Commander-in-Chief to accept the bombardment of the port, which he was most reluctant to undertake, as a *pis aller*. Cunningham's rejoinder, written in his own hand, is marked 'Not what was sent but similar':

I do not think that Dudley Pound was capable of such double dealing in his relations with his Commander-in-Chief and especially with me . . . Nor was there any necessity for him to gain his wishes by subterfuge; it was within the powers of the Admiralty to order the fleet to bombard.

He would have known the agony of mind the sacrifice, not so much of the Barham, but of well over 1,000 officers and men unwarned of their fate, would cause to the Commander-in-Chief and he would never have adopted a ruse of this sort . . .

After all these years my view remains as it was at the time; that is amazement at the ill-advised and reckless irresponsibility of those who ordered the bombardment or its alternative.

The operation was successful but by good luck and the favour of Providence only. We might well have suffered complete disaster and lost the whole fleet. A disaster such as happened only a few months later in those self-same waters to *Neptune* and the cruisers with her. And this at a time when convoys were passing in rapid succession backwards and forwards to Greece and a strong Italian fleet was within striking distance.

Retirement had not diminished Cunningham's readiness to open up with his main armament if he thought the target worthwhile. *A Sailor's Odyssey* if not quite so outspoken as this private letter did not attempt to disguise the author's feelings at what he felt to have been unwarrantable intrusions into his proper field of professional competence or insulting aspersions on his courage. Mr Churchill acknowledged the gift of a copy and expressed his expectation of pleasure in reading it but perhaps unsurprisingly there is no further communication from him on the subject. He would certainly have been aware that Cunningham was one of the half-dozen Admirals of the Fleet headed by Chatfield who twice petitioned the Admiralty to enquire into the dismissal of Admiral Sir Dudley North on grounds that were generally thought in the service to have been unsatisfactory. Churchill seems to have felt this to be a personal attack: he was in any case determined that North should be refused a hearing. It is not difficult to detect the smouldering of past resentment in this, probably their final, exchange of letters in June 1954.

The occasion of it was a characteristically generous attempt by Cunningham to have Admiral Sir John Edelsten who had served under him both at sea and in the Anti-Submarine Department of the Admiralty raised to the rank of Admiral of the Fleet. No objection was raised on professional grounds but the Treasury, ever vigilant over precedent and protocol, pointed out disapprovingly that ten was the traditional number of Admirals of the Fleet and that there were already ten occupants of the rank. Knowing that this type of argument was usually a red rag to the Churchillian bull, Cunningham sent him a draft letter to the Admiralty and asked his support. The reply from 10 Downing Street is dated 15 June 1954:

My dear Andrew

I should very gladly forward your letter to the Admiralty if you so desire. On the general question of numbers of Admirals of the Fleet it is not a question of saving a few hundred pounds but of not lowering the prestige of the title by having too many.

I think Vian was hardly treated in being driven out of the service. In my opinion he fought the finest naval action of the war – four light cruisers against two or three Italian battle cruisers. I am sorry that I allowed him to be so treated.

Yours vy. sincerely

Winston S. Churchill

The allusion to Vian was not irrelevant but double-edged. He had commanded the Home Fleet from 1950 to 1952. On relinquishing that appointment he had, unusually, gone straight on to the retired list and had been, even more unusually, promoted Admiral of the Fleet. Cunningham and Vian were personally and professionally very close to each other. Both were fighting leaders of the highest quality. Neither saw himself or was seen by others as an outstanding performer in staff work or administration. Indeed Vian's fierce intolerance of publicly expressed difference of opinion would have made him a very difficult colleague in the Chiefs of Staff Committee. And it was exceptional to promote a man Admiral of the Fleet unless he had served as First Sea Lord.

Be that as it may there can be little doubt that this letter was intended to put the victor of Taranto and Matapan in his place – with a vengeance. Cunningham took his time over answering, which he did on 28 June with studied moderation: 'I have not entirely lost hope that you will intervene on Sir John Edelsten's behalf. I am sure his addition to the numbers of the Admirals of the Fleet would certainly cause no loss of prestige to the rank, indeed quite the contrary and his services to the country fully merit his advancement.

I fully agree with you that Vian's action off Sirte was the finest naval action of the war; in the Mediterranean at the time we were all very proud of it.'

Some of the differences that had arisen in the war had a happier issue. Mountbatten had several times incurred A.B.C.'s displeasure for what seemed to him pushfulness or arrogance. When in 1953 his name had been put forward as a candidate for the succession to the post of First Sea Lord, Cunningham had objected. A year later, on 22 October 1954, he wrote to the First Sea Lord with a complete retraction. Mountbatten, he was sure, was the man for the hour. Finally, nearly three years later, the North affair was at last settled under Macmillan's premiership. Its resolution prompted a touching letter from Chatfield, thanking him for his support: 'Please my dear Andrew call me Ernle. I do value your friendship. It was you who sustained me in my old age.'

Cunningham's long reflection on the conduct and lessons of the Second World War was stimulated not only by writing his own memoirs or by his attempts to secure justice for brother officers and mercy for Esteva and Laborde. Stephen Roskill, whose official history *The War at Sea* is at all points worthy of its subject, constantly questioned and corresponded with him and was given the full run of his mind as well as his papers. Their exchanges led Roskill to suggest in a letter dated 2 September 1953 that Cunningham should formulate his views on current defence policy. Both men were agreed that wars of necessity were fought on policies arrived at long before the opening shot was fired. The time to get policy right was when the country was at peace. 'The trouble to-day,' wrote Roskill, 'is that the American atom bomb enthusiasts lead NATO by the nose and we, with our maritime tradition and needs, get a very poor hearing.'

This resulted in an undated document of some two or three thousand words that is worth quoting at some length because it crystallizes Cunningham's thinking on the great matter of his life. He starts by emphasizing the point that defence policy is formed in peace and relates it to the democratic constitution under which we live – and which he has no wish to alter.

So long as our form of Government remains as it is, we shall never be fully prepared for war. This is bound to mean that an aggressor nation will at first possess the strategic initiative while our own strategy must, of necessity rather than from choice, initially be defensive. During that phase we must preserve these islands intact and strengthen the defences of our bases oversea; we must gain time to change our economy from a peace to a war footing, and we must at all costs keep open the sea and air transport lanes upon which our continued survival entirely depends. This is but the well-established principles of a maritime strategy brought up to date.

A maritime strategy is not, and never has been, a method of waging war by naval forces alone. It can be more fully explained by saying that we devote our main resources to an adequate control of the seas and skies to enable us ultimately to move our forces to strike the enemy in one or more theatres where we shall have him placed at a military disadvantage. At the same time we deny to the enemy the ability to do the same thing. In every phase and every aspect of a maritime strategy the Royal Air Force has to-day a tremendous part to play – but by no means the only part.

Cunningham here drew on the course of the Second World War to illustrate his argument. He then turns to the impact of nuclear bombs:

The argument that a bigger or better weapon has changed such principles as these is as old as weapons themselves, and again and again it has been shown to be fallacious. [In this connection he had already cited the 'strategic' bombing of Germany instead of using our air power to defend the convoys on which everything depended.] We believe that even if atomic bombing were to obliterate all but a few contestants on both sides it might still be necessary for the survivors to settle the final issue by land combat; and that we must still regard it as a primary duty of the other two Services to place the soldier where he is needed, when he is needed – as he certainly will be – and with the supplies which he must have to fight.

No one who has twice in his life-time come through the ordeal of seeing Britain's sea communications very nearly severed and the country brought to the verge of defeat can ever forget the simple, but easily forgotten, saying that 'if we lose at sea we lose the war'. To which may now be added if we lose the war in the air we lose the war.

One strategy covers the whole.

It is this grasp of the strategic unities that had made him so determined an opponent of supreme commands. Any service chief worth his salt must recognize the interdependence of all military effort. It was this that had inspired the sacrifice of so much of his own striking power in the Mediterranean to rescue or support the soldiers. It was this that made him see red when the true cost of victory was falsified. 'It's wonderful how the Army wins the war by itself.' He never for a moment believed that the navy could.

Retirement was neither as impoverished nor as useless as he had in his darker moments suspected. Life at Palace House, Bishops Waltham pursued an even tenor, but there was enough of public service and public honour to give it dignity and point. Cunningham had been admitted to the Order of Merit in 1946. He had been elected Rector of Edinburgh University in 1947, an office in which some of his successors would hardly have been his choice as shipmates. His place in the national life was better recognized by his appointment as Lord High Steward at the coronation in 1952. Besides the elucidation of the story of events in which he had played so notable a part he devoted considerable energy to improving the prospects of the Royal Corps of Naval Constructors, serving as President of the Institution of Naval Architects from 1948–1951. He did much for charity, especially when it was directed towards the young as in the case of the Gordon Boys' Home. His membership of the Order of the Thistle and of the Queen's Bodyguard for Scotland had perhaps heightened his pride in his ancestry. He accepted with enthusiasm the Presidency of the Royal Naval Pipers Society.

Next to the Thistle the Scottish connection that moved him most was his service in 1950 and 1952 as Lord High Commissioner to the General Assembly of the Church of Scotland, of which his grandfather had been Moderator. What was his religion and what part, if any, did it play in his life? His own natural reticence about the intimacies of life leaves the matter untreated. There is nothing about it in his autobiography and precious little in his letters. From this we may safely conclude that it was undemonstrative. It might further be deduced from the weekend entries of his diary, which never record a visit to a place of worship, that it was inconsiderable. But this might prove too exclusive a reliance on literary evidence. The tone of his mind suggests very strongly that he shared the insight of the Psalmist into the perceptions of those who occupy their business in great waters, an insight memorably restated in our time by Eric Newby in *The Last Grain Race*. He certainly refers solemnly and not conventionally to the workings of Providence. His chaplain in the *Queen Elizabeth* who as Bishop of Norwich preached his funeral sermon thought his personal religion profound. In such a nature profundity makes obvious sense. He could not be shallow or frivolous. And if the profundity was not religious, what was it? Sceptical? Disenchanted? Tragic? None of them seems to match. Perhaps the surest evidence, as with so much to do with Cunningham, is to be found in action. As soon as his ships had returned to harbour after the Battle of Matapan the Commander-in-Chief ordered Prayers of Thanksgiving to be said throughout the fleet. At nine o'clock that Tuesday morning the Prayer pennant was hoisted and the collect to be used after Victory or Deliverance from an Enemy was recited on every quarter-deck in the presence of the whole ship's company. 'O Almighty God, the Sovereign Commander of all the world, in whose hand is power and might which none is able to withstand . . .'

To be private in their religion was common to both Cunningham and Fisher, whose daily attendance at the Eucharist was not advertised and whose general course of life does not suggest ideas of the devout. But, as one stands back to look at them, how little else

183

they had in common. An engaging, exuberant boyishness perhaps. Jan Morris in an article on Fisher which one wishes had grown into the book originally intended singles out the enchantment, the mischief of his smile. So it was with an old woman who had survived from the palmy days of Marienbad where Fisher had regularly taken the waters. Asked if she recalled the Admiral 'her answer was immediate, short and convincing. "Jacky Fisher!" she said. "What a face that man had."' So might the bright blue eyes and ruddy complexion of Cunningham have been recalled as a symbol of cheerfulness and exhilaration.

But such resemblance is as chaff before the gale of antipathy. That Cunningham was aware of this is suggested by a remark in one of his letters to Stephen Roskill: 'I have always taken great satisfaction in that the naval operations of this last war were not marred by the disputes and jealousies between the Commanders in 1914/18 that were so deplorable and did so much harm.' The habitual opening words of a Trafalgar Night speech, 'Brother Officers!' came from his heart. They can hardly have done so from Fisher's who reintroduced into the officer corps the hateful spirit of the gang and the clique that Nelson had done so much to exorcize.

To recapitulate, the many other points at which the two men stood at opposite ends of the scale would by no means produce the kind of clear-cut result by which the Day of Judgment is conventionally represented. Fisher listened with interest to innovative suggestions from junior officers; Cunningham told them to shut up. Fisher was ready to question every accepted opinion or practice; Cunningham firmly believed that the old ways were the best. Fisher's prophetic, seer-like vision was extraordinary: many of his ideas, submarine battleships for instance, were a couple of generations ahead of the technology of his time; Cunningham contemplated technical advance with misgiving and dislike. Fisher saw at once that any major decision about the defence of the country was necessarily a political decision and that therefore politicians and other sources and centres of political power, the Crown, the Press, must be cultivated if the navy was to have any say in what such decisions might be. It was in any case a pursuit that he wholeheartedly enjoyed. Cunningham hardly got beyond a cold distaste for politicians as such and an even more extreme repugnance to contact with the Press. Fisher's readiness to question the established order in everything led him not only to encourage the development of new weapons but to improve the pay and conditions of the lower deck. Cunningham was instinctively against making naval life more comfortable and shrank from anything that smacked of popularity-seeking with the lower deck. He was not a snob; he much valued his long friendships with sailors who had served with him in many commissions. But the relationship was essentially paternal and, in the eyes of the generation that was joining the navy when he was First Sea Lord, old-fashioned.

And so one could go on. But by now it is plain enough that if either of these two remarkable men are to be compared with Nelson, Cunningham bears far and away the closer resemblance. Quite apart from moral qualities such as loyalty and straightforwardness, from admired abilities as a seaman and shiphandler, from high achievement as a fighting leader, it is impossible to imagine either man finding his full scope in any other profession. Nelson and Cunningham were born naval officers; born not in the hereditary sense that has played such a part in our maritime and naval history but born in some mysterious sense of being fore-ordained.

Fisher, on the other hand, could have risen, must have risen, to the top of a dozen careers, several of them far better fitted to his genius for publicity, his love of disconcerting the *bien-pensants*, his passion for intrigue, his joyous unscrupulousness, his charm, his wit, his vision, his executive ruthlessness. In spite of picturesque rhetoric about the educative effects of taking in sail on a dirty night in the South Atlantic it was on dry land among the busy hum of men that his extraordinary talents won their just recognition. It was fortunate for Lord Beaverbrook and Lord Northcliffe that they did not find him as a competitor in Fleet Street.

Notes

1 Marder, Arthur, *Fear God and Dread Nought: the letters of Admiral of the Fleet Lord Fisher of Kilverstone*, iii, p. 635.
2 ibid, ii, p. 292.
3 ibid, p. 114.
4 ibid, p. 155.
5 ibid, i, p. 302.
6 ibid, ii, p. 318.
7 Fisher [Lord Fisher of Kilverstone], *Memories*, p. 149.
8 Marder, ii, p. 364.
9 ibid, i, p. 181.
10 ibid, pp. 214–5.
11 ibid, ii, p. 467.
12 ibid, pp. 87, 88.
13 ibid, iii, p. 466.
14 Fisher, p. 102.
15 Pollen, Anthony, *The Great Gunnery Scandal*, pp. 56–7.
16 Roskill, Stephen, *Hankey*, i, pp. 102–3.
17 Marder, iii, p. 56, fn. 4.
18 ibid, p. 488.
19 ibid, ii, p. 461.
20 ibid, iii, p. 468.
21 ibid, pp. 326–7.
22 ibid, ii, p. 425.
23 ibid, pp. 451–2.
24 ibid, p. 459.
25 ibid, pp. 459–60.
26 ibid, iii, p. 480.
27 Roskill, i, p. 155.
28 Lloyd George, David, *War Memoirs* (new edition 1934), i, p. 135.
29 Marder, ii, p. 432.
30 ibid, i, p. 247.
31 ibid, pp. 261–2.
32 Fisher, p. 260. (I have been unable to find confirmatory evidence of this charming scene; and *Memories* is not by any means a wholly reliable source.)
33 Letter written by Keyes to Churchill, 22 December 1940, *The Keyes Papers* (Navy Records Society), iii, p. 134.

Index

Styles and titles are generally given as in the text. Sometimes they are amplified to assist identification. Abbreviations used in Index: C. = Cunningham; F. = Fisher; Med. = Mediterranean.

based on, 112, 121, 123–4, 143; German air offensive against, 122; George VI's visit to, 144

Marder, Professor Arthur, 50; *From the Dreadnought to Scapa Flow*, 14; *Fear God and Dread Nought* (editor), 14, 39

Marshall, General George, 137–8

Mary, Queen (George V's consort), 40

Matapan, Battle of Cape (1941), 75, 100, 109–11, 130, 179, 183

Midway, battle of, 101

Monck, General George, 1st Duke of Albemarle, 86, 108

Montgomery, Bernard, Field Marshal Lord, 33, 116, 145, 158, 160–1, 173, 174

Morgan, Charles, *The Gun Room*, 59

Morris, Jan, 184

Mountbatten, Lord Louis, 70, 134, 163 &n, 173, 174, 180

Munich Crisis (1938), 76

Mussolini, Benito, 72

mutiny, 119

NATO, 180

Nelson, Admiral Lord, 11, 12, 13, 14, 15, 19, 23, 24–5, 68, 72, 90, 108, 171, 185

Neptune, HMS (cruiser), 98, 177

Newby, Eric, *The Last Grain Race*, 183

North, Admiral Sir Dudley, 94, 178, 180

North Africa, 99, 102, 121; Allied landings in (1942), 138–43, 158, 160

nuclear weapons, 181

Ocean, HMS, sailing vessel, 31

Oliver, Admiral Sir Geoffrey, 70–1, 120

Oran, 142; British action against French Fleet in (1940), 84, 85–96, 103

Orion, HMS, 120

'Overlord', Operation (invasion of France, 1944), 149, 157, 158

Pacific Fleet, British, 164–5

Pacific War, 149–51, 156, 157

Pack, Captain S.W.C., biography of C. by, 13, 124–5, 126

Palace House (C.'s home at Bishops Waltham), 73, 182

Pantellaria *see* 'Workshop', Operation

Parker, Admiral Sir William, 12

Peiho forts, Battle of the, 22, 38

Perth, HMS, 120

poison gas, 166

Pollen, Anthony, *The Great Gunnery Scandal*, 34–5

Pollen, Arthur, fire-control system affair, 34–5, 37–9

Port Said, 82

Portal, Air-Chief Marshal Sir Charles, 69, 153, 154, 159, 161–2

Potsdam Conference (1945), 161, 168

Pound, Admiral Sir Dudley, 75–6, 77, 82, 90, 99, 106, 116, 120, 121, 127–8, 133, 134–5, 177; First Sea Lord, 103; and Operation 'Workshop' 104; resigns as First Sea Lord, 134, 146; death, 134, 146–7

Pound, Lady, death of, 134, 146

Power, Admiral Sir Manley, 62–3, 110

Pridham, Vice-Admiral Sir Francis, 66

prize money, 172

Pumphrey, Captain Nigel, 139–40

Quebec Conference (1944), 146, 149, 155–6

Queen Elizabeth battleships, 48, 123, 162, 183

Queen Mary, 155

Ramsay, Admiral Sir Bertram, 143, 149, 156, 157, 160, 161

Rawlings, Admiral Sir Bernard, 11

Renown, HMS, 149

Rhodes, Cecil, 58–9

Riccardi, Admiral, 75, 98

Richelieu, French battleship, 141

Richmond, Admiral Sir Herbert, 36

Robeck, Admiral de, 64, 106

Roberts, Frederick, Field-Marshal Lord, 59–60

Rodney, HMS (battleship), 70–1

Rommel, Field-Marshal Erwin, 99, 121, 122, 143

Roosevelt, President Franklin D., 134, 137, 142, 155–6

Rosebery, Lord, 37

Roskill, Stephen, 35, 93, 184; *The War at Sea 1939–45*, 11, 13, 94, 117–18, 144, 146–7, 180; *Churchill and the Admirals*, 132–3, 134, 162

Royal Air Force, 99, 109, 112, 162

Royal Corps of Naval Constructors, 182

Royal Naval Pipers Society, 182

Royal Sovereign, HMS (battleship), 98

Russia (USSR), German invasion of (1941), 122; convoys to, 149, 164; Yalta Conference (1945), 168–9

Salerno landings, 145–6, 158

Scharnhorst, sinking of (1943), 149, 163

Scorpion, HMS (destroyer), 63, 175

Scott, C.P., 33, 45–6, 52

Second Opium War, 22

Second World War (1939–45), 58, 61, 62–3, 75, 78–170